WEATHERING THE STORM

WEATHERING THE STORM

Independent Writing Programs in the
Age of Fiscal Austerity

EDITED BY
RICHARD N. MATZEN JR.
AND MATTHEW ABRAHAM

UTAH STATE UNIVERSITY PRESS
Logan

© 2019 by University Press of Colorado

Published by Utah State University Press
An imprint of University Press of Colorado
245 Century Circle, Suite 202
Louisville, Colorado 80027

 ASSOCIATION
of UNIVERSITY
PRESSES The University Press of Colorado is a proud member of
the Association of University Presses.

The University Press of Colorado is a cooperative publishing enterprise supported,
in part, by Adams State University, Colorado State University, Fort Lewis College,
Metropolitan State University of Denver, Regis University, University of Colorado,
University of Northern Colorado, Utah State University, and Western State Colorado
University.

∞ This paper meets the requirements of the ANSI/NISO Z39.48–1992 (Permanence of
Paper)

ISBN: 978-1-60732-894-0 (paperback)
ISBN: 978-1-60732-895-7 (ebook)
https://doi.org/10.7330/9781607328957

Library of Congress Cataloging-in-Publication Data

Names: Matzen, Richard N., Jr., editor. | Abraham, Matthew, 1972– editor.
Title: Weathering the storm : independent writing programs in the age of fiscal austerity
/ edited by Richard N. Matzen Jr. and Matthew Abraham.
Description: Logan : Utah State University Press, [2019] | Includes bibliographical refer-
ences and index.
Identifiers: LCCN 2019018445 | ISBN 9781607328940 (pbk.) | ISBN 9781607328957
(ebook)
Subjects: LCSH: English language—Rhetoric—Study and teaching (Higher)—Economic
aspects—United States. | English language—Rhetoric—Study and teaching (Higher)—
Political aspects—United States. | Writing centers—Economic aspects—United States.
| Writing centers—Political aspects—United States. | Education, Higher—Economic
aspects—United States. | Global Financial Crisis, 2008–2009.
Classification: LCC PE1405.U6 W43 2019 | DDC 808/.042071173—dc23
LC record available at https://lccn.loc.gov/2019018445

Cover illustration © Sergey Nivens/Shutterstock.com

CONTENTS

Foreword

AN INVITATION TO READ FOR RESILIENCE

Louise Wetherbee Phelps

As I have noted earlier (Phelps 2016), it has been immensely difficult to track the rise of independent writing units in American higher education with reliable and stable data. But we know enough to dispel some of the cloud of skepticism and pessimism that accompanied their early development. If we take the organization IWDPA (Independent Writing Departments and Programs Association) as a proxy for their growth, the movement for independence began to gather steam in the early 1990s, when a special interest group emerged at the Conference on College Composition and Communication. By 2009, it had gathered sufficient momentum to formalize the organization now known as IWDPA, which has standing-group status at CCCC and is affiliated with the Council of Writing Program Administrators. In 2016, using IDWPA and other sources, I counted around sixty self-declared programs as well as others in planning; but, as this volume illustrates, "the status of independent writing programs in the aggregate is [still] in constant flux as units transition between different stages: new formations, mergers, internal reorganization, reincorporation into larger units, even suspension in limbo through indecision or ambiguity" (Phelps 2016, 334). Our best opportunity to learn about such units has therefore been through self-reported case studies, of which this collection is third in a series, preceded by *A Field of Dreams* (O'Neill, Crow, and Burton 2002) and *A Minefield of Dreams* (Everett and Hanganu-Bresch 2016). Together, as they follow some programs over decades, these volumes are beginning to construct a longitudinal picture of the robustness of independent writing units during times of turbulence and disruptive change in higher education.

This collection not only updates a cumulative history of independent writing units, but adds a valuable new dimension by asking how they have responded to a common external shock—the "Great Recession"

DOI: 10.7330/9781607328957.c000a

of 2008. The editors solicited accounts of how independent units of varying ages fared under the conditions of "financial austerity," not just during the immediate crisis but as its consequences played out over a decade. By identifying this event as a major stressor for these programs, they offer the opportunity to inquire, in concrete instances, whether and how IDWPs have been *resilient* in the face of adversity. I'd like to explore here how readers can take up this invitation to "read for resilience," and raise questions about the conditions, qualities, and attitudes that may afford it.

The concept of resilience, which originated in the study of ecosystems (Holling 1973), has been taken up with variable meanings by disciplines in the ecological and social sciences to explain how dynamic systems respond to change that threatens their stability (Downes et al 2013). For present purposes, I'll draw my definition from interdisciplinary studies of integrated social-ecological systems (SESs), as developed by Folke and his colleagues (2010). They propose a framework for "resilience thinking" that highlights three aspects of systems' response to adversity: *persistence, adaptability*, and *transformability*.

To "persist" as a system through times of constant pressure on higher education, IDWPs can adapt by making adjustments (for example, cutting less crucial functions, delaying plans for growth or innovation, and redirecting energies to institutional priorities) that allow them "to maintain the same identity" (Folke et al. 2010, table 1). Adaptation might involve becoming more like traditional fields and their departments (for example, developing a vertical curriculum) or, alternately, tailoring a program to fit closely to the unique culture of an institution. However, severe systemic shocks, especially to the larger systems in which a program is embedded (the institution, the state, national or global markets for education, and so on), can overwhelm its ability to adapt. In this case, programs can navigate the crisis by accepting the inevitability of radical change and trying to steer it in positive directions. "Transformability" refers to the capability of a program, as a dynamic system, to negotiate major "shifts in perception and meaning, social network configurations, patterns of interaction among actors including leadership and political and power relations, and associated organizational and institutional arrangements" (Folke et al. 2010, para. 16). In these circumstances, resilience thinking requires not just adaptation but also the opposite: invention, risk taking, and experimentation with bold and unconventional designs. Programs must actually break down and give up the old resilience of a stable state and an established trajectory, and rebuild resilience around a new identity, in a new "stability landscape," with a new trajectory for its future (para. 25). That spirit is captured perfectly in this quotation from Traci Zimmerman's chapter on James Madison University: "What we are working on now is not how to redefine ourselves based on our past identities but how to define and develop 'the new'" (this volume, 64).

Although this volume sets out to explore responses to a specific crisis—what Folke and his coauthors (2010, para. 14) call "specified resilience"—contributors illustrate the point that such stressors seldom occur in a vacuum; typically, they interact with other stresses and challenges, like student enrollment drops or demographic changes, that require "general resilience" in responding to multiple shocks, since efforts to deal with one in isolation can be counterproductive.

By understanding "persistence" (of a system, of its identity) in terms of both adaptation and transformation, the resilience framework offered by Folke and his colleagues (2010, para. 23) "broadens the description of resilience beyond its meaning as a buffer for conserving what you have and recovering what you were" to "incorporate the dynamic interplay of persistence, adaptability and transformability across multiple scales." At best, programs may deliberately initiate transformations, especially at small scales, in order to "shape the outcomes of forced transformation occurring at larger scales," like the financial crisis of 2008. Such initiatives may adopt an adaptive approach to shape "transformation trajectories," "facilitating different transformative experiments at small scales and allowing cross-learning and new initiatives to emerge, constrained only by avoiding trajectories that the SES does not wish to follow" (Folke et al. 2010, paras. 9–10). One might even argue that independent writing programs as a group constitute a trans-institutional example in which the discipline of writing studies has initiated a transformation trajectory for all writing programs through multiple experiments with independence at local sites (see Burton 2002).

It's tempting for me to analyze how these chapters display resilience across the whole range—from adaptations that preserve a relatively stable state to textbook cases of radical transformation—but I will leave it to readers to map out this spectrum. Instead, I want to raise some questions that cluster around the relations among resilience, identity, and independence.

I couldn't help but wonder what made these units so resilient, even when faced with apparent loss of their treasured "independence." In particular, what difference does "independence" make when units are put under stress? I brainstormed some possible reasons for their resilience, which I don't have space to explore here: among them, institutional knowledge among writing faculty (a systems-level understanding of institutions, realism about the forces that affect them); entrepreneurial leadership styles that facilitate boldness, innovation, and openness to change (Ross 2016); habits, experience, interest, and rhetorical astuteness in collaborating with other disciplines, reflecting both the interdisciplinary nature of the field itself (Bazerman 2011) and the "institutional logic" of writing programs (Phelps 1991); ability to align with institutional priorities, given writing units' typical involvement in institutional reforms and innovations; and a fluidity and multiplicity of identity (in the discipline and its programs) that allows writing units to shift functions or emphases nimbly to fit contexts and circumstances.

In almost all cases, the qualities that seem to me to afford resilience, while rooted in the nature and history of writing studies as a discipline and observable in embedded writing programs, are greatly enhanced by independence. "Independence" as attributed to a writing program or department defines it as having an identity of its own, which gives it a degree of agency *as itself.* That means, for example, it has a name, appears in institutional policies and documents, has a seat at the table in various forums, has a say in what happens within it and to it, can interact and speak directly with administrative offices and other disciplinary units, and can track data about its activities through institutional record keeping. I witnessed one example of a writing program so deeply embedded that, despite administering a universal writing requirement, it had none of these kinds of recognition—no name as a "program," no access, no official presence on campus or trace in institutional data. It was literally invisible to the institution. So, independence means having enough distinctiveness and coherence as a function and a unit to be an institutional actor, able to enter freely into various relationships with other institutional actors and units.

From a developmental perspective, though, identity in an individual or an institutional unit is never static; it is fluid, multiple, and highly negotiated. An independent writing unit that adapts doesn't really "stay the same"—it grows and changes—but in some sense along the same trajectory or within a "landscape" that is relatively stable. But when it transforms, it is hard to pin down exactly what continues, since that process may change its name, personnel, leadership, curriculum, structure, and everything else that gave the original unit its identity. There is no objective way to define a core identity that persists, yet (as some chapters here report) there is a sense of identity sustained through transformational transitions. I suggest that continuity of identity in resilient transformation lies in the process itself and the historical memory it creates among participants and at the institution. It is a process of experiencing and actively contributing to the transition, during which a writing unit's identity is (re)negotiated, stabilized through concrete actions that are reified materially and textually (things like budgets, policy documents, appointment letters, name changes, committee structures, space allocation)—all deliberately directed toward rebuilding a new resilience. Identity persists even through multiple cycles of such changes, which are often volatile, as long as it has subjective, intersubjective, and objective correlates in both public memory and records.

The question that preoccupies those here faced with the greatest changes—especially forced transformations—is losing an identity they equate with independence. As contributors to this volume understand, all programs and departments are ultimately interdependent. Programs and departments are always part of larger units like schools and colleges, but most of their institutional agency occurs at the program-department level. Many departments (including English departments) are multidisciplinary at heart, and must negotiate to what degree they will operate that way versus negotiating interdisciplinary activities or functions. From reading these chapters, I believe resilient transformation means, for an independent unit, not necessarily that it remains "free-standing" in the literal sense of "alone," but that it continues through a new interdependent identity to be able to function as an institutional actor, both *within* its new configuration (if merged or part of a larger structure) and *as* that new structure, if that is the level at which agency is defined. As some examples here suggest, having once been independent is likely to enhance (both phenomenologically and institutionally) the ability for a writing unit to maintain a distinct identity and agency even when reconfigured in (or as) a merged department or a school.

I'd like to end by calling for more research to guide our understanding of resilience, within a larger effort to document and theorize the development of independent writing units longitudinally. On the research side, we need more objective empirical perspectives to supplement the phenomenological perspectives in these narratives, which are important for understanding perceived identity and resilient behaviors. As Larry Burton (2002) rightly pointed out, independent writing units are educational experiments—individually diverse and highly context-dependent—that will inevitably experience both successes and failures. But to assess the phenomenon as a whole, we need to study the evolution of a range of independent units through multiple cycles of change and in comparison to the status quo—embedded programs—over the same time scale. Criteria like vulnerability to financial austerity, conditions for labor, or opportunities for curricular innovation are relative: who has asked how dependent programs fared during the Great Recession or how resilient they are under stress? That point is made spectacularly in John Ruszkiewisz's chapter here on the toxic climate at the University of Texas at Austin that prompted Maxine Hairston (1985) to compose her famous "Breaking Our Bonds" speech. On the theory side, we are fortunate that Michelle Cox, Jeffrey Galin, and Dan Melzer (2018) have recently published a book that integrates resilience thinking with several other systems theories into a framework for theorizing sustainable writing across the curriculum (WAC) programs. Not only do they lay out a comprehensive "whole systems" theory, but they translate it into a methodology and strategies for practice. While their perspective is prospective—how to build and sustain programs—it is just as useful for retrospective and longitudinal analysis; and while it is specified for WAC programs, it applies equally well to independent writing units (many of which have WAC/WID [writing in the disciplines] origins or missions). We can build on their splendid start to develop deeper theoretical understandings of independence, interdependence, identity, and resilience in the units that house writing studies.

REFERENCES

Bazerman, Charles. 2011. "The Disciplined Interdisciplinarity of Writing Studies." *Research in the Teaching of English* 46 (1): 8–21.

Burton, Larry. 2002. "Afterword: Countering the Naysayers: Independent Writing Programs as Successful Experiments in American Education." In *A Field of Dreams: Independent Writing Programs and the Future of Composition Studies*, ed. Peggy O'Neill, Angela Crow, and Larry Burton, 295–300. Logan: Utah State University Press.

Cox, Michelle, Jeffrey R. Galin, and Dan Melzer. 2018. *Sustainable WAC: A Whole Systems Approach to Launching and Developing Writing across the Curriculum Programs*. Urbana, IL: National Council for English Education.

Downes, Barbara J., Fiona Miller, Jon Barnett, Alena Glaister, and Heidi Ellemor. 2013. "How Do We Know about Resilience? An Analysis of Empirical Research on Resilience, and Implications for Interdisciplinary Praxis." *Environmental Research Letters* 8 (014041): 1–8.

Everett, Justin, and Cristina Hanganu-Bresch, eds. 2016. *A Minefield of Dreams: Triumphs and Travails of Independent Writing Programs*. Fort Collins: WAC Clearinghouse and University Press of Colorado.

Folke, Carl, Stephan R. Carpenter, Brian Walker, Marten Scheffer, Terry Chapin, and Johan Rockstrom. 2010. "Resilience Thinking: Integrating Resilience, Adaptability, and Transformability." *Ecology and Society* 15 (4): 20.

Hairston, Maxine. 1985. "Breaking Our Bonds and Reaffirming Our Connections." *College Composition and Communication* 36: 272–82.

Holling, C. S. 1973. "Resilience and Stability of Ecological Systems." *Annual Review of Ecology and Systematics* 4 (1): 1–23.

O'Neill, Peggy, Angela Crow, and Larry Burton, eds. 2002. *A Field of Dreams: Independent Writing Programs and the Future of Composition Studies*. Logan: Utah State University Press.

Phelps, Louise Wetherbee. 1991. "The Institutional Logic of Writing Programs: Catalyst, Laboratory, and Pattern for Change." In *The Politics of Writing Instruction*, ed. Richard Bullock and John Trimbur, 155–70. Portsmouth, NH: Boynton/Cook Heinemann.

Phelps, Louise Wetherbee. 2016. "Between Smoke and Crystal: Accomplishing In(ter)dependent Writing Programs." In *A Minefield of Dreams: Triumphs and Travails of Independent Writing Programs*, ed. Justin Everett and Cristina Hanganu-Bresch, 321–50. Fort Collins: WAC Clearinghouse and University Press of Colorado.

Ross, Valerie C. 2016. "Managing Change in an IWP: Identity, Leadership Style, and Communication Strategies." In *A Minefield of Dreams: Triumphs and Travails of Independent Writing Programs*, ed. Justin Everett and Cristina Hanganu-Bresch, 245–68. Fort Collins: WAC Clearinghouse and University Press of Colorado.

WEATHERING THE STORM

Introduction

LOOKING TOWARD AN (INTER)DISCIPLINARY FUTURE?

Richard N. Matzen Jr. and Matthew Abraham

To begin at the beginning, *Weathering the Storm: Independent Writing Programs in the Age of Austerity*'s chapter 1 offers a detailed account of the events and considerations inside the University of Texas Austin's Department of English that prompted Maxine Hairston's 1985 landmark Conference on College Composition and Communication (CCCC) address, a call for writing programs to separate from English departments.

Thereafter, the history of independent writing programs (IWPs) was portrayed in 2002 in *A Field of Dreams: Independent Writing Programs and the Future of Composition Studies* (O'Neill, Crow, and Burton). IWPs' history was extended in 2017 with the publication of *A Minefield of Dreams: Triumphs and Travails of Independent Writing Programs* (Everett and Hanganu-Bresch). Among other things, our book *Weathering the Storm: Independent Writing Programs in the Age of Austerity* adds to this ongoing history and conversation by addressing the question that concludes *A Field of Dreams*' introduction: "Can we, as independent writing programs, shift our gaze toward the future in such a way that we are able to participate in the university that is emerging" (O'Neill, Crow, and Burton 2002, 18).

When viewed as a whole, the thirteen case studies herein suggest that generally speaking, IWPs possess successful futures possibly because they are participating in dialogues between university departments and offices that may develop into multi- or interdisciplinary relationships (Repko, Szostak, and Phillips Buchberger 2013) and perhaps evolve into alliances. Our case studies, moreover, are researched longitudinal narratives into how independent writing departments (IWDs), not just programs, fit into a disciplinary landscape—or a landscape of fields and disciplines—greater than English or writing studies. This essential *fitting* into the greater university, we think, signifies that writing studies are far from standalone programs or departments existing in an institutional

DOI: 10.7330/9781607328957.c000b

hierarchy. In particular, we posit that these case studies may indicate that IWDs/IWPs will increasingly rely on diverse disciplinary perspectives, while also maintaining their financial durability.

All thirteen case studies discuss negotiating the Great Recession that started in 2008. Herein, the preponderance of evidence suggests that IWDs/IWPs are typically indispensable to institutions because of first-year writing courses regardless of, or possibly because of, economic times. As several scholars including Sharon Crowley (1998) and Susan Miller (1991) have documented, the first-year writing course(s) has had a contentious history in the university precisely because of its role in the production of institutional subjectivities that comply with authoritative figures and texts. The courses' relationship with literature is complicated, needless to say, in that these first-year *writing* courses could be teaching *reading* literature or could be teaching content less applicable to the writing tasks students will do later at the university or on the job. Furthermore, as read in *Conceding Composition, a Crooked History of Composition's Institutional Fortunes* (Skinnell 2016, back jacket), first-year writing courses may "help institutions solve political, promotional, and financial problems" not directly related to how best to teach students how to write well.

Nevertheless, during difficult economic times, IWDs/IWPs may not only be economically protected by first-year writing courses, the IWPs/IWDs may also expand writing studies' curricula and programs by creating writing majors or minors, by modifying existing writing curricula, or by creating (or expanding) English as a second language (ESL) programs or writing centers, for example. Such writing studies' activities, incidentally, may reinforce retention if not expand student enrollment. This book's case studies, subsequently, function as a collective account for how small, medium, and large IWPs/IWDs fared not only during the Great Recession but also during recent years when states have had smaller budgets for education, when fewer students have enrolled at universities, and when the national economy seems to have recovered from the Great Recession.

Weathering the Storm: Independent Writing Programs in the Age of Austerity may also be read as an alternative narrative compared to *A Minefield of Dreams* (Everett and Hanganu-Bresch 2017). Therein, its editors suggest that IWPs have "a difficult path" (5) in the future and still struggle to have writing accepted as a discipline (11). The alternative narrative, presented herein, is that IWPs' successes usually, but not always, outpace their challenges even during difficult financial times. In so doing, a question emerges, not about whether writing studies is a discipline but about how best to describe the discipline of writing studies interacting with other disciplines.

THIRTEEN LONGITUDINAL CASE STUDIES

In general, this book's thirteen longitudinal case studies represent older IWDs/IWPs: twenty-five years is the average age of the case studies herein. The age of each is determined by subtracting its birth year from 2018 (see table 0.1). In each chapter, the case study's history extends to 2016 or 2017. The case studies consist of five small universities (1,275 to 6,824 students), four medium universities (9,384 to 15,196 students), and four big universities (19,396 to 39,619 students).

Collectively, the thirteen case studies (or chapters) suggest that not only can IWDs/IWPs fare well during difficult financial times but also during such times, they adjust writing curriculum to better address student needs and market conditions. In other words, the long history of these IWDs/IWPs suggests that if the future reflects the past—in spite of the ebbs and flows of finances, student enrollment, and curricular innovations—numerous ways exist for IWDs/IWPs to perpetuate their financial health.

A DEFINITION FOR AN INDEPENDENT WRITING PROGRAM?

Our book, *Weathering the Storm,* includes seven case studies of writing departments (chapters 2, 4, 6, 8, 10, 11, and 14), five case studies of independent writing programs (chapters 3, 7, 9, 12, and 13), and a case study of an entire school devoted to writing studies (chapter 5). Two writing departments, however, recently joined English departments to help their universities save administrative costs (chapters 3 and 9). Nevertheless, in keeping with a traditional definition of an IWP, eleven of the thirteen case studies herein have a point in their past in which an independent writing program was born by separating from an English department.

But separating from an English department does not make all independent writing programs alike. For instance, five chapters herein demonstrate how an IWP may be founded on first-year writing (chapters 2, 3, 5, 6, and 10); two depict how an IWP may start as a writing across the curriculum (WAC)/writing in the disciplines (WID) program (chapters 12 and 13); and one portrays an IWP as founded on both a first-year composition and a WAC/WID program (chapter 14). Two other chapters tell the story of how IWPs may merge with other IWPs within an institution (chapters 5 and 14).

Table 0.1. Thirteen independent writing departments or programs

Birth Year	University	University's Size: Student Numbers	Chapter Author(s)
1972	Loyola University Maryland	4,004 (small)	Moore and O'Neill
1975	St. Edward's University	4,023 (small)	Clements, Loewe, and Rist
1985	Maxine Hairston's CCCC address, "Breaking Our Bonds and Reaffirming Our Connections"		
1986	Syracuse University	15,196 (medium)	Agnew and Schell
1987	University of Minnesota Duluth	9,837 (medium)	Beard and Park
1987	University of California Santa Barbara	20,607 (big)	Adler-Kassner and Sorapure
1992	University of Texas Austin	39,619 (big)	Longaker, Charney, Davis, and Batt
1993	University of Arkansas at Little Rock	9,384 (medium)	Harris and Jensen
1995	James Madison University	19,396 (big)	Zimmerman
2002	University of California Davis	28,384 (big)	Thaiss and Whithaus
2003	University of Pennsylvania Philadelphia	9,726 (medium)	Ross, Wehner, and LeGrand
2005	Woodbury University	1,275 (small)	Matzen
2008	Hofstra University	6,824 (small)	Gaughan
2009	University of Wisconsin–Superior	2,362 (small)	White-Farnham

Note: Gray highlighting indicates independent writing departments; the others are independent writing programs (with the exception of James Madison University). The Birth Year column indicates when the writing program became independent from an English department or when the independent writing department or program was created. Information on the universities' sizes came from COLLEGEdata (2017).

Given such diversity in IWPs' roots, should we be surprised that some IWDs/IWPs find themselves enjoying multi- or interdisciplinary relationships or looking toward multi- or interdisciplinary horizons? Perhaps not, if we assume that often English departments themselves look like sites for disciplines (or fields) meeting each other. Yet, have we had any consistent language to describe the relationships among literature, writing centers, English teacher education, creative writing, basic writing, WAC/WID, linguistics, foreign languages, ESL programs, and professional/technical writing—all of which may possibly exist within one English department? A good question may be, how can we best describe such a variety of interrelations between English programs?

We may consider, as this book does, the usefulness and applicability of these terms: inter-, multi-, and transdisciplinarity, as they are defined by interdisciplinary scholars (Repko, Szostak, and Phillips Buchberger 2013, 35). We may consider, for example, that the writing center is an interdisciplinary activity for integrating two disciplinary perspectives—education and writing studies—"to construct a more comprehensive understanding of the problem," which is how best to conduct a one-on-one tutorial. Or we may consider that the relationships between literature and writing studies may be interdisciplinary or multidisciplinary.

Multidisciplinary means that "the study of a complex issue" is done from "the perspective of two or more disciplines by drawing on their insights but making no attempt to integrate them. Insights are juxtaposed . . . not integrated" (Repko, Szostak, and Phillips Buchberger 2013, 35). This may describe how literature and writing studies relate to each other. Or, as suggested earlier, theirs is an interdisciplinary relationship that constructs "a more comprehensive understanding of the problem," which may be defined as literacy (Repko, Szostak, and Phillips Buchberger 2013, 35).

Why not consider, furthermore, the possibility that neither an interdisciplinary nor a multidisciplinary relationship between literature and writing studies guarantees a happy or a troubled relationship (see chapters 3 and 9 for examples of these relationships). We should remember, too, that at the department or program level, personalities are known to define these relationships as well. But, generally speaking, and considering that close relationships may exist between literature and writing studies, it may be that writing studies has more often defined itself in relationship to literature (or English) as compared to the opposite case.

Subsequently, when reading this book, two good questions may be, first, do IWDs/IWPs possess multi- or interdiscplinarity qualities as a natural outgrowth caused by being located within English departments at some point, or were these qualities inherent in writing studies in the first place? Second, are the chapters' authors revealing a tendency to follow multidisciplinary and interdisciplinary strategies that help establish IWDs/IWPs more firmly in the institutional landscape? Said another way, in the long life of IWD/IWP, how definitive is its relationship to an English department and to other disciplines? In eleven chapters of this book, separating from the English department, however, seems to be only one event among other equally significant events that shape an IWD/IWP.

Considering IWDs/IWPs as multi- or interdisciplinary sites may not be particularly profound. For example, we can return to *A Field of Dreams* (O'Neill, Crow, and Burton 2002) and find mention of interdisciplinarity therein. Some of its chapters may be read as representing interdisciplinary perspectives as definitive or central to an IWP:

- **Chapter 1:** Harvard University's "independent and interdisciplinary" Expository Writing Program, led by revered writing studies scholars (O'Neill and Schendel 2002, 194)
- **Chapter 3:** Metropolitan State University, where IWP majors were characterized as fulfilling an "interdisciplinary" curriculum (Aronson and Hansen 2002, 54)
- **Chapter 4:** San Francisco State University's Technical and Professional Writing program that included "interdisciplinary breadth" (Rehling 2002, 73)
- **Chapter 9:** University of Minnesota's Program in Composition and Communication (an IWP) that was returned to the Department of English, resulting in the lessening of interdisciplinary qualities in the IWP (Anson 2002, 155)

In other words, *A Field of Dreams*' editors Peggy O'Neill, Angela Crow, and Larry Burton (2002) may be tacitly endorsing interdisciplinarity as a legitimate, if not desirable, basis for an IWP. Therein, reporting on national survey results regarding IWPs, author and editor Peggy O'Neill (189–92) says that significant numbers of IWPs characterized themselves as "interdisciplinary." Also, author and editor Angela Crow in her chapter 12 (216), after citing "disparate values" between literature and composition faculty in an English department, wrote that the "historical tensions between the two areas continued to grow as composition became an increasingly independent and interdisciplinary field." *Weathering the Storm* may be understood as confirming that latter thought.

PART I. ADDING WRITING MAJORS OR MINORS
DURING THE GREAT RECESSION

Part I introduces readers to IWDs/IWPs that created writing majors or minors within the context of the Great Recession (2007–9). As is the case for part II, part I chapters are arranged from the oldest IWD/IWP at the beginning to the youngest IWD/IWP at the end. In part I, four chapters tell us that *during* 2008 and 2009, IWDs/IWPs were adding a writing major or minor to their existing curricula as a response to the Great Recession or as an extension of previous enrollment growth. Examples follow.

In 2007, a new writing and rhetoric major, built on a successful writing minor, begins at Syracuse University (chapter 2), and in 2009, a new writing major and new Department of Writing Studies debuts at the University of Minnesota Duluth (chapter 3). Also, regarding the University of Texas Austin, the basis of chapters 1 and 4, Professors Longaker, Charney, Davis, and Batt report that the "rhetoric and writing undergraduate major officially began in the fall of 2006 . . . The program had enrolled 21 majors in January 2007, 140 majors in October 2008, 214 in September 2010, and 218 as of September 2016" (chapter 4).

Another positive development during the Great Recession, regarding new writing majors and minors, occurs at James Madison University (chapter 5). Specifically, Professor Zimmerman informs us, "On Valentine's Day 2008, the Writing and Rhetoric Program (W&R) was administratively merged with the Institute for Technical and Scientific Communication (ITSC), and the School of Writing, Rhetoric and Technical Communication (WRTC) . . . was born." How meaningful is this merger? "Before the merger, ITSC offered an undergraduate major and minor as well as a master's degree; W&R offered only a minor. After the merger, W&R faculty inherited a major and a master's program (literally) overnight, while the small TSC faculty of five gained twenty-two new full-time colleagues" (Zimmerman, chapter 5).

Nevertheless, the smaller universities—Loyola University Maryland (chapter 8), University of Wisconsin–Superior (chapter 7), and Woodbury University (chapter 6)—tell complicated stories about the Great Recession's relationship to problematic IWP enrollments and finances.

Regarding the University of Wisconsin–Superior (chapter 7), Professor White-Farnham writes that the university's enrollment actually increases in 2008 because of students seeking job retraining, a reaction to the Great Recession. The next year, 2009, the IWP leaves the Department of English and starts a writing minor. However, also during 2009, the IWP endures staff reductions, a restructuring of chairs' release time, and a merger of the IWP with Library Sciences. The merger is an attempt to save administrative costs. The year after that, 2010, the University of Wisconsin–Superior's enrollment reaches a high point, but enrollments decline thereafter. Professor White-Farnham observes that the IWP faculty "did little explicitly to acknowledge or enhance students' economic expectations of their college degrees until [faculty's] own financial stability was threatened." Eventually, the Great Recession means that this IWP "reevaluated the purpose and value of [the] curriculum," implemented a new curriculum, and grew the writing minor to a point that a writing major was successfully proposed in 2015.

Like the University of Wisconsin–Superior, Woodbury University initially experiences an enrollment increase starting in 2008 and lasting until 2012 (chapter 6). A shortage of seats for students in the University of California, California State University, and California community college systems drives this increase to the point that Woodbury University, a nonprofit private university, experiences a historically high enrollment in the fall of 2012. In 2013, however, when California restores funding to its university and community college systems, Woodbury's enrollment steadily drops, reaching a low point in the fall of 2017. Because of enrollment losses—caused by the state of California recovering from the Great Recession—Woodbury's IWD successfully proposes a professional writing major in 2014. In the fall of 2016, however, Woodbury's IWD's new major only attracts five students. Subsequently, in 2018, the upper administration considers suspending the professional writing curriculum. Hoping to prevent that, the IWD presents positive financial evidence based on the stability of first-year writing courses' enrollment; a curricular, cost-saving alliance with the Department of Communication; and a steady increase in professional writing minors. The future of the professional writing curriculum is uncertain at the time of this writing.

PART II. ADJUSTING EXISTING CURRICULA IN RESPONSE TO THE GREAT RECESSION

Although it did not add a writing major or minor during (or because of) the Great Recession, another IWD leveraged its Writing Center to create greater financial security during the recession (chapter 14). As told by Professor Gaughan regarding Hofstra University, 2008 and 2009 were the first two years of the Department of Writing Studies and Composition's existence. While a hiring freeze impairs some ambitions, the department, "drawing on in-house expertise," creates "an undergraduate peer tutor program and a four-credit practicum course" (Gaughan, chapter 14). The upper-division course enrolls students reliably because its completion leads to Writing Center employment. At the same time, the Writing Center grows "by attending to the needs of core constituencies" (Gaughan, chapter 14). Total Writing Center appointments subsequently exceed "5,000 appointments per year" (Gaughan, chapter 14), remarkable considering that approximately 6,500 to 7,000 total students attend Hofstra University. Professor Gaughan also comments that "English language learners [made] up about one-third of the total tutoring appointments."

Another IWP, moreover, found greater security during the Greater Recession without adding a major or minor at that time but by addressing the needs of increasing numbers of English language learners. As reported by Professors Whithaus and Thaiss (chapter 12), "The University Writing Program (UWP) at UC Davis experienced tremendous growth; this growth affected all areas of the Writing Program but was particularly pronounced in an increased number of English as a second language (ESL)–focused courses." The professors explain, too, that by embracing professional multi- and interdisciplinary approaches, since the recession the IWP "has greatly expanded its full-time (including tenure-line) research and teaching faculty, doubled course offerings, and developed a successful undergraduate professional writing minor and PhD emphasis in writing and rhetoric" (Whithaus and Thaiss 2017).

However, during the Great Recession, other IWDs/IWPs suffer varying degrees of short-term losses during which they reevaluate and modify their writing curriculum and programs for long-term gains. These IWDs/IWPs successfully adjusted, in other words, to effectively address new economic times. IWDs/IWPs at Loyola University Maryland (chapter 8), St. Edward's University (chapter 9), the University of California Santa Barbara (chapter 10), and the University of Arkansas Little Rock (chapter 11) exemplify this theme.

For example, at the beginning of the Great Recession, Loyola University Maryland's long-established IWD sees its "enrollments dip considerably" (Moore and O'Neill, chapter 8). Then, responding to the Great Recession, the department revises its writing major curriculum in 2009–10 to include "more rhetoric and professional writing options" (Moore and O'Neill, chapter 8). But only beginning in 2015, eight years after the Great Recession's start, do student numbers begin to increase, thanks mostly to the extensive long-term efforts of faculty recruiting students.

Also illustrating how challenging financial times may inspire curricular and recruitment innovations, the IWD at St. Edward's University (chapter 9) learns to use its writing program alumni as a resource to guide reconstructing the writing major and as a means for recruiting students and locating new resources for them. The program succeeds after a rebuilding period, as well.

The IWD at the University of Arkansas at Little Rock (chapter 11), furthermore, suffers short-term setbacks during the Great Recession while planning successful long-term changes. Specifically, the Department of Rhetoric and Writing, also profiled in *A Field of Dreams*, revises its BA degree and begins to embed technology and multimedia into its curriculum in 2008. But, while that positive curricular revision goes forth, the Great Recession also means that the department's proposal for a new PhD program in rhetoric, professional writing, and digital media is "put on indefinite hold" (Harris and Jensen, chapter 11) because of the economic pressure created by declining enrollment. As the undergraduate writing major's enrollment declines in 2008, the department fortunately experiences an enrollment increase in its master's writing program. This latter development eventually leads to the success of offering both undergraduate and graduate degrees in fully online formats.

Regarding curricular adjustments and the Great Recession, Professors Adler-Kassner and Sorapure write, in reference to the IWD at the University of California Santa Barbara, "Coming out of the Great Recession, Writing Program faculty numbers had shrunk only slightly and only through 'natural' attrition such as retirements. The program avoided the layoffs, workload reductions, and furloughs that affected other departments and universities" (chapter 10). The professors also explain that the Great Recession means the writing program "discontinued offering all non-GE-status courses . . . restructured its upper-division course offerings," and offered "new GE courses" (Adler-Kassner and Sorapure, chapter 10), all of which was done successfully.

Finally, in this book's case studies, one IWP simply endures the Great Recession. Professors Ross, Wehner, and LeGrand (chapter 13) summarize its effect on their writing program this way: "The Critical Writing Program of the University of Pennsylvania was . . . sufficiently stabilized and integrated into the university such that the financial crisis [the Great Recession] affected our program no differently from the rest of the university."

HOW DOES INTERDISCIPLINARY FIGURE INTO OUR WORK?

In other words, sometimes poor economic conditions and lower enrollments cause IWDs/IWPs to create inspired curricular innovations, with success usually, but not always, defining the innovations' results. As will be noted shortly, interdisciplinary connections are often an important, if not definitive, characteristic of the curricular innovations found in this collection of case studies. Before summarizing that point, however, a brief exploration of the term *interdisciplinary* is needed, given how usage makes this term problematic, if not ornery.

One problematic feature found in how the term is used is that interdisciplinary has contrastive, if not vague, meanings across university departments and curricular descriptions. A tension exists, in other words, in how individual departments (or disciplines) may define interdisciplinarity and how educational organizations (e.g., a university, professional organization, accrediting bodies) external to the department define the term. For example, interdisciplinarity does *not* have the same specific meaning in the disciplines of writing studies, engineering, medicine, and education. Another problematic feature of interdisciplinarity is that in rhetoric and writing studies, it has multiple meanings that encourage either loose or multiple tight (too tight?) definitions of the term. To say that interdisciplinarity is the combining of two disciplines, for example, may not adequately define how a rhetorician may define the term from a historical perspective.

Hoping to create a tighter definition herein, the coeditors looked into interdisciplinary studies and found what may appear to be a tighter definition of interdisciplinarity as well as its relatives, multi- and transdisciplinarity (Repko, Szostak, and Phillips Buchberger 2013). Some writing studies colleagues may interpret this move as ignoring, diluting, or betraying our discipline (for example, see the reflection in chapter 3). Other colleagues may see this move as attempting to oversimplify how writing program administrators decide what to do (for example, see the reflection in chapter 10). Professors Adler-Kassner and Sorapure (chapter 10) describe interdisciplinarity's difficult situation this way:

> [The] brief history of the UCSB Writing Program shows that interdisciplinary, multidisciplinary, and transdisciplinary approaches are all in play in the development of an independent writing program. There is no "correct" way for a program to define its relation to other disciplines or reach out to other academic departments and units.
>
> Rather, an array of contextual factors—economic, curricular, institutional, students, and staffing—determine the most strategic and effective ways for an IWP to define itself and make connections across campus, and these factors are constantly in flux.

In the postscript, the introduction's final section, we return to the complications swirling around interdisciplinarity. Thereafter, chapter authors address these complications, as well as complications that exist around the term *independent*, by writing a reflection—a response to the postscript—that ends each chapter.

According to *Weathering the Storm* professors, multi-, inter-, and transdisciplinarity bring diverse prospects to writing studies. For example, just because an IWD possesses such inclinations does not mean other departments will reciprocate. In chapter 2, Professors Agnew and Schell write, "the vitality of our [writing] program has depended upon our awareness of the intrinsic interdisciplinarity of writing and rhetoric scholarship and pedagogy," but they also examine their "university's tendency to create silos of expertise" and to market these disciplinary silos, which in turn fosters "competing perspectives about literacy"—not conducive to creating a broader interdisciplinary view of writing, much less to sharing resources.

How multi- or interdisciplinarity may or may not mediate discussions between writing and literature faculty is noteworthy as well. In chapter 3, Professors Beard and Park describe what happens when their IWD is forced to (re-)join an English department. In their reflection they write, "While re-merger has been described as an opportunity to institutionalize interdisciplinarity, it has been experienced as an exercise of power," that is, interdisciplinarity is irrelevant.

Nevertheless, other faculty groups have different collegial experiences, and describe the diverse scholarship among English professors as *interdependent* as well as permeated by interdisciplinary concepts. Chapter 13's professors write in their reflection that "everything is inter-/multi-/transdisciplinary-specific." Then, after characterizing Ken Bruffee as an inter-/multi-/transdisciplinary figure, they emphasize that their writing programs find "new ways to express [their] glorious interdependence." After writing that their academic, creative, and professional writing faculty members are "interdependent," chapter 12's professors also write that their faculty are "engaged in debating the ways we translate inter- and multidisciplinary frameworks into curricula and degree programs." Likewise, chapter 4's professors characterize the relationships among an independent writing (and rhetoric) department, a writing center, and a digital lab as "interdependent" and add that their "proposals to partner with departments in other colleges to develop multidisciplinary writing courses were received favorably at both the college and university levels" (chapter 4's reflection).

Considering these thoughts, multi-, inter-, and transdisciplinarity are perhaps useful terms for us. In chapter 7's reflection, Professor White-Farnham writes that he has "come to appreciate the fact that writing belongs to the university through its capacity for transdisciplinarity—or participating in the larger political project of public higher education in creative ways alongside other disciplines." Mining this possibility, chapters 4, 7, 8, and 10 claim that interdisciplinary concepts help their IWDs/IWPs broaden their universities' mission. Chapters 5, 7, 8, and 10 also demonstrate how interdisciplinary concepts can support universities' general education curriculum. Chapters 2, 8, and 10, moreover, include interdisciplinarity as a basis for first-year writing curricula.

In other words, interdisciplinary concepts may be understood as underpinning an IWD/IWP and making its work relevant to other departments and disciplines. For instance, at James Madison University (JMU), three independent writing programs were joined, with the result that faculty shared an "interdisciplinary status" to create one curriculum (chapter 5). Then, their "major courses [were] also affiliated with several multidisciplinary minors at JMU as well as with two study abroad programs." Their "Community Based Learning courses (a requirement for all our majors)" connected their "students in valuable and visible ways to the surrounding community," perhaps exemplifying transdisciplinarity.

Interdisciplinary concepts may be understood not only as a means to create greater engagement with the university but also as a way to secure an IWD's/IWP's bottom line. Consider the reality, discussed in chapter 8, that a writing major may exist alongside an interdisciplinary writing major (i.e., half the courses being in a discipline outside the writing curriculum). Or, consider chapters 9 and 10, which illustrate interdisciplinarity as a basis for successful writing minors. Furthermore, consider chapters 7 and 9, which demonstrate how courses in a writing major may attract students from other majors, given the multi- or interdisciplinary nature of the major's writing courses. Chapter 6 ends with that thought by describing combining professional writing and communication curricula in the hope of saving the professional writing curriculum from being suspended. Chapter 14 also discusses multi- or interdisciplinary concepts as emerging within an IWD.

Finally, we may review chapter 11, in which the idea is proposed that while interdisciplinary concepts may be useful now, a fully online IWD may mean that eventually all disciplinary boundaries will be removed because of the effects of networking in the future.

POSTSCRIPT

In *Weathering the Storm*, it's difficult to define a "model" for an IWP or IWD because any particular one—given the average age of twenty-six years for all the IWPs/IWDs herein—embodies more than one model, hence more than one definition. This quality, combined with the research adage not to over-generalize from any one particular case that's contextualized by local conditions, means that drawing reliable conclusions about the nature of IWPs/IWDs is tricky at best.

Not surprisingly, any study of IWPs/IWDs entails complications. For instance, an IWP/IWD, in order to be successful, likely has to change over time, which complicates the notion of an "independent" writing program or department. As read in these chapters, no writing program or department is ever truly independent of, or liberated from, the working conditions of a university. That is, every writing program or department is dependent on others for funding: student enrollments, university finances, state financial support, federal student financial aid, and so on. Also, as read herein, a writing program's independence or liberation from an English department may be just one significant event among others shaping any writing program that has sustained over decades. A good question to ask, subsequently, may be whether a narrative built around independence from an English department is the most constructive way to frame *independent writing programs* as notable.

Weathering the Storm, we think, makes an argument for understanding the *independence* of a writing program or department to mean a willingness to define writing studies in relation to other disciplines and departments. Such willingness may be cast into high relief during times of economic scarcity. That said, we wonder if IWPs/IWDs are steadily pushing toward interdisciplinarity and if this pressure necessitates a greater examination of the relationship between writing studies and interdisciplinary studies.

In *Interdisciplinary Research Process and Theory*, interdisciplinary scholar Allen Repko makes a distinction between a "discipline" and "studies." According to him, "Every established discipline has a universally recognized core of knowledge, and this core is subdivided into specific courses called a curriculum" (Repko 2011, 7), which for us may be a way to describe literature as a discipline. Then, with interdisciplinary studies in mind, Repko (2011, 8) writes, "'Studies' is an integral part of interdisciplinary studies because it refers to a wide array of knowledge domains, work, and educational programs that involve crossing disciplinary domains." This may be a way to understand *writing studies*, in contrast to literature, as possessing a similar "wide array of knowledge domains" (e.g., writing, rhetoric, sociolinguistics), "work" (e.g., writing program administration work), and "educational programs" (e.g., literacy programs and writing across the disciplines and writing in the disciplines programs) "that involve crossing disciplinary domains."

In other words, we may explore independent writing programs, and writing studies in general, as sites that may include interdisciplinary, multidisciplinary, or transdisciplinary features. If we go down this path, interdisciplinary scholars Allen Repko, Rich Szostak, and Michelle Phillips Buchberger may be our guides. For instance, they tell us, "Multidisciplinarity is the study of a complex issue, problem, or question from the perspective of two or more disciplines by drawing on their insights but *making no attempt to integrate them*. Insights are juxtaposed (i.e., placed side by side) and are added together, but not integrated" (Repko, Szostak, and Phillips Buchberger 2013, 35).

Here, our guides might ask us if multidisciplinarity describes writing center tutorials, in which *writing* meets a *discipline*. Referring to tutorials, they may note that neither tutors nor tutees expect to have fully integrated writing into a given discipline as a result of their work. Our guides may ask, too, are writing center studies typically discussed in terms of multidisciplinary activities?

Our interdisciplinary guides, perhaps our colleagues, may also inform us about transdisciplinarity: "Transdisciplinarity is the cooperation of academics, stakeholders, and practitioners to solve complex societal or environmental problems of common interest with the goal of resolving them by designing and implementing public policy" (Repko, Szostak, and Phillips Buchberger 2013, 36). Hence, our guides may ask whether our support for the Common Core, or our understanding of the Core Competencies, as defined by Western Association of Schools and Colleges accreditors, are really transdisciplinary activities. Would we agree? If so, would we study transdisciplinarity to enhance our participation in the Common Core and to better integrate the teaching and learning of the Core Competencies on our campuses?

As we consider answers, our guides—the interdisciplinary scholars—drop us off at the conference center and ask whether we think literacy and writing studies may benefit from interdisciplinary insights. But seeing that we are exhausted, they leave us with their company's business card, which reads: "Interdisciplinarity is the study of a complex issue, problem, or question from the perspective of two or more disciplines by drawing on their insights and *integrating them*. The interdisciplinary process is used to construct a more comprehensive understanding of the problem. The object of inquiry may be an intellectual or a real-world issue" (Repko, Szostak, and Phillips Buchberger 2013, 35).

Inside the conference center, each of us pockets the business card.

An ESL specialist asks, "Do you think that our interdisciplinary colleagues—our guides—are asking us to study their knowledge of interdisciplinarity, multidisciplinarity, and transdisciplinarity to better focus our understanding of the problem, how best to teach writing?"

A colleague with an EdD degree says, "That's a huge question. But it might be helpful if we knew, before entering into a campus collaboration, if a particular discipline is more open to a specific interdisciplinary, multidisciplinary, or transdisciplinary perspective. Or we could ask ourselves if at the graduate level, rhet/comp students should study business courses to enhance their qualifications to become WPAs. Then we would have to decide if that curricular relationship is fully integrated, an interdisciplinary approach, or more like just setting the two subjects side by side, a multidisciplinary approach."

"At the undergraduate level, professional writing and media studies programs," says the ESL specialist, "might have to decide a similar question. Is theirs a multidisciplinary or an interdisciplinary relationship?"

As the two scholars talk into the night, they realize they're not so different. But, after all, they both work in the same independent writing program.

REFERENCES

Anson, Chris M. 2002. "Who Wants Composition? Reflections on the Rise and Fall of an Independent Program." In *A Field of Dreams: Independent Writing Programs and the Future of Composition Studies*, ed. Peggy O'Neill, Angela Crow, and Larry Burton, 153–69. Logan: Utah State University Press.

Aronson, Anne, and Craig Hansen. 2002. "Writing Identity: The Independent Writing Department as a Disciplinary Center." In *A Field of Dreams: Independent Writing Programs and the Future of Composition Studies*, ed. Peggy O'Neill, Angela Crow, and Larry Burton, 50–61. Logan: Utah State University Press.

COLLEGEdata, your online college advisor. 2017. http://www.collegedata.com.

Crow, Angela. 2002. "Wagering Tenure by Signing on with Independent Writing Programs." In *A Field of Dreams: Independent Writing Programs and the Future of Composition Studies*, ed. Peggy O'Neill, Angela Crow, and Larry Burton, 213–29. Logan: Utah State University Press.

Crowley, Sharon. 1998. *Composition in the University: Historical and Polemical Essays*. Pittsburgh: University of Pittsburgh Press.

Everett, Justin, and Cristina Hanganu-Bresch, eds. 2017. *A Minefield of Dreams: Triumphs and Travails of Independent Writing Programs*. Fort Collins: WAC Clearinghouse and University Press of Colorado.

Hairston, Maxine. 1985. "Breaking Our Bonds and Reaffirming Our Connections." *College Composition and Communication* 36 (3): 272–82.

Miller, Susan. 1991. *Textual Carnivals: The Politics of Composition*. Carbondale: Southern Illinois University Press.

O'Neill, Peggy, Angela Crow, and Larry Burton, eds. 2002. *A Field of Dreams: Independent Writing Programs and the Future of Composition Studies*. Logan: Utah State University Press.

O'Neill, Peggy, and Ellen Schendel. 2002. "Locating Writing Programs in Research Universities." In *A Field of Dreams: Independent Writing Programs and the Future of Composition Studies*, ed. Peggy O'Neill, Angela Crow, and Larry Burton, 186–211. Logan: Utah State University Press.

Rehling, Louise. 2002. "Small but Good: How a Specialized Writing Program Goes It Alone." In *A Field of Dreams: Independent Writing Programs and the Future of Composition Studies*, ed. Peggy O'Neill, Angela Crow, and Larry Burton, 50–61. Logan: Utah State University Press.

Repko, Allen. 2011. *Interdisciplinary Research Process and Theory*. 2nd ed. Thousand Oaks, CA: Sage.

Repko, Allen, Rich Szostak, and Michelle Phillips Buchberger. 2013. *Introduction to Interdisciplinary Studies*. Thousand Oaks, CA: Sage.

Skinnell, Ryan. 2016. *Conceding Composition, a Crooked History of Composition's Institutional Fortunes*. Logan: Utah State University Press.

Whithaus, Carl, and Chris Thaiss. 2017. "Abstract for 'A Complex Ecology: The Growth of an Independent Writing Program in the Aftermath of the Great Recession.'" Unpublished manuscript.

1

DOCUMENTS OF DISSENT
Hairston's "Breaking Our Bonds" in Context

John J. Ruszkiewicz

About halfway through "Breaking Our Bonds and Reaffirming Our Connections," her 1985 chair's address to the Conference on College Composition and Communication, Maxine Hairston faces a Rubicon moment. Describing the imbalanced relationship in college English departments between teachers of writing (largely responsible for service courses) and a ruling class of literary scholars and critics she compared just a few paragraphs earlier to the bureaucrats of Imperial China, Maxine coolly observes: "In addressing the mandarins, we are not in a rhetorical situation." She then reminds her audience of the conditions Lloyd Bitzer had set down for one: "There has to be an *exigence* that can be modified by discourse, and there has to be an *audience* of persons who are capable of being influenced by that discourse" (Hairston 1985, 277).

Maxine (Hairston 1985, 273) was always attuned to the circumstances of teachers of writing across the country, from big programs and small, specifically acknowledging in her speech the work of instructors she had met "in places like Parsons, Kansas, or McAllen, Texas, or Montgomery County, Maryland." But there can be little doubt, either, that when she finally calls on her professional colleagues in rhetoric and composition to consider separating from departments of English, she is drawing upon experiences with her home department at the University of Texas at Austin: "Fighting the literature faculty often makes you feel like you have invaded China. You can mount an all-out assault and think you are making an impression, but when the smoke clears, nothing has changed. The mandarins are untouched."

More than thirty years later, memories of the exigence that created "Breaking Our Bonds" grow fainter in Austin, but they are preserved in documents produced in and around the Department of English between 1979 and 1986. In the space available here, I can't usefully

DOI: 10.7330/9781607328957.c001

recount the whole struggle Maxine alludes to, but the very shape and genres of the texts produced in those years help clarify the context of Hairston's address and the caliber of its achievement.

An abstract of the period might focus on James Kinneavy's ambitious, but ultimately doomed, effort in the early 1980s to restructure the sequence of composition courses at the University of Texas, but a headline from a *Chronicle of Higher Education* news story published just a month after Maxine's 4Cs address is more succinct: "50 Lecturers Lose Their Jobs in a Dispute over How—and If—Writing Can Be Taught" (Heller 1985, 23). To address the needs of a fast-growing population, Kinneavy had proposed a curriculum reform to guarantee students at the University of Texas training in writing throughout their undergraduate careers. At its core would be a formidable upper-division course called English 346K "Writing across the Disciplines," which would replace a required second-semester lower-division writing class. The university community initially embraced the reform, wrote it into course catalogs, and officially approved it on May 28, 1981, after several years of deliberation.

But as this new writing across the curriculum (WAC) program ground toward implementation (suffice it to say, mistakes *were* made all around), senior literature faculty in English pondered its implications. Innovative WAC courses, most of them far removed from the literary canon, would have to be created, supervised, evaluated, and—most worrying of all—staffed. Because graduate students could not teach these upper-division offerings, many more adjunct faculty would be needed at a time when university rules gave instructors with full-time appointments voting rights in a department. Teaching mostly writing courses, these adjuncts would, it was feared, inevitably align with the rhetoric program, and the English department's center of gravity might shift.

The navel of the state had been touched.

The ensuing conflict would play out in brutal curriculum debates, battles over the status of "temporary" faculty, governance wars, and the eventual cancellation of the entire WAC program. When the smoke cleared, the rhetoric program was once again safely in the hands of faculty trained in literature, and those who had sided with Kinneavy—Maxine, of course, included—found themselves consigned to a sort of internal exile. Mandarins untouched indeed.

Predictably, the earliest documents I reviewed for this piece (from roughly 1979–81) are unremarkable minutes from departmental or University Senate meetings, dutifully reported in conventional formats by impartial secretaries. These blurred but durable mimeographs are precisely as civil and collegial as one would expect from academic bodies heavily engaged in the sober business of rethinking a university curriculum. After all, discourse theorist James Kinneavy, who had succeeded Maxine Hairston as director of Freshman English at UT-Austin in 1975, enjoyed wide respect among his literary colleagues—especially since his proposals promised cuts in the number of writing courses required. (At a May 1980 departmental meeting, chair Joseph Moldenhauer predicted staffing reductions of "roughly 20–25 percent" under the new program.)

In many ways, the years leading up to Maxine's speech were heady times for rhetoric faculty at Texas. The English department had unanimously endorsed a graduate concentration in rhetoric and, in quick sequence, hired Lester Faigley, Steve Witte, and, slightly later, Greg Myers. Graduate students attracted to the program in these years included Hugh Burns, Susan Jarratt, David Jolliffe, Thomas Miller, and Cindy Selfe, among others. Erika Lindemann and James Berlin trod the halls as scholars-in-residence. And with a stellar job-placement record, the new PhD concentration in rhetoric looked golden. English faculty even created a Departmental Senate in 1981 to lend voice in governance to graduate students and an expanding pool of adjunct instructors who were previously not represented at ordinary faculty meetings or on the Executive Committee.

Yet, even in this halcyon time, there were doubts and fears about the Kinneavy reforms. For instance, Charles Rossman, a professor of British literature, used a two-page, single-spaced psychomachia to frame his dissent. In the undated "'Position Paper' for Freshman Composition Committee—Format I," distributed to a course committee working on the new writing program, God—who presciently threatens to build a "Writing Lab" or "Department of Rhetoric and Composition"—spars with a far more likable Satan, the champion of literary study. The demon's arguments echo *Gorgias*: "You have converted a concern with the forms and strategies of writing into a subject matter"; "Let us teach our students *literature*, give them genuine content, and then help them find the best ways to write about that" (ca. 1980).

Rolling out in pilot sections in 1981–83, the E346K courses were soon putting pressure on institutional resources. Documents from those years relating to the English program grow more impromptu and harried, as administrators wrestle with prerequisites, test scores, exemptions, and credit transfers, all of which point to one conclusion: the full writing reform will be *far* more massive than anyone had envisioned. On October 9, 1982, the famously irascible linguist James Sledd weighs in on the matter, siding with neither the literature faculty nor writing program administrators like Kinneavy and Hairston (whom he will later deride as "boss compositionists"). Directing four pages of questions to the president of the university, Sledd (1982a) describes the new English program and revised admissions requirements as "gross mistakes" designed "to make U.T. Austin still more nearly a preserve for affluent and exploitative Anglos." By December 7, his complaint to the University Council has grown to nineteen single-spaced pages, with its conclusion underscored: "*There is evidence that the new requirements in English are intended as a step toward the complete abolition of freshman composition*" (Sledd 1982b). A floodgate opens. Over the next several years, the minutes of both the Department of English and the University Council (later rechristened as the Faculty Senate) record lengthy and ever-more-rancorous debates about every aspect of the new writing program—and the motives of those favoring or opposing it.

Before long, conventional departmental meetings, and the minutes they generate, aren't enough. Professors, lecturers, and graduate students—now acting individually or in groups—offer statements and schemes of their own. Faculty mailboxes become a preferred venue for debate, a sort of paper intranet, stripped of the courtesies of face-to-face encounters. Every matter relating to the writing program (almost the department's only concern, it seems) is parsed and analyzed like a Donne poem. When the employment status of the adjunct lecturers becomes a focal point in 1983–84—chiefly as a result of a move to deny them voting rights by reducing them to three-quarters time—a paper war ensues, paralleling acrimonious meetings of the regular faculty as a whole and of the separate Departmental Senate. A five-person committee of that senate offers a document on the status of lecturers; several lecturers prepare alternative statements of their own, one with "have patience . . ." in its title; Kinneavy distributes two items, one captioned "Lecturers: Victims of Both Systems"; I discover that I, too, wrote a document on the lecturer problem, long forgotten.

Meta-discourse about department meetings proliferates: for instance, a faculty member distributes a lengthy ditto to annotate the details of a motion he'd already offered verbally; a graduate student on the Departmental Senate, rather than speak at a meeting certain to "be dominated by emotional speaking and lobbying," circulates a printed rationale for his views. Civilities are disappearing and the department knows it. The minutes from a departmental meeting of April 19, 1984, include this telling passage:

> Hairston commented that a change of culture had taken place in the department over the years with a rise of new classes (an elite professoriate and slave laborers). She asserted that the current situation at UT and

other schools across the nation constitutes a threat to the profession as a whole, that it weakens the professoriate, that it is sexist, and that it harms both undergraduate and graduate students in the Department.

A colleague calls her remarks "undocumented" and "counterproductive."

After long months of escalating and embarrassing wrangling, the dean of liberal arts, Robert D. King, reacts to the turmoil in the English department by placing it in receivership. On September 14, 1984, he writes to its new chair, W.O.S. Sutherland, that "in accordance with common University policy, departmental authority is vested solely in the Chairman and the Executive Committee" (King 1984). Three days later, members of the rhetoric interest group compose and narrowly circulate a document summarizing the actions of the English department and of Sutherland, in particular, aimed at diminishing the teaching of writing. I do not recall if the item went beyond the group, and the specific purpose of the document is not specified, but its final lines focus on two possibilities:

Establishing a Center for Writing within the Department?
Splitting off into a Department of Language and Rhetoric?

Other materials from the period suggest that Dean King *was*, in fact, exploring the logistics of creating a separate unit of writing in fall 1984. Maxine and I discussed that option regularly, but James Kinneavy showed no enthusiasm for it.

In the spring term, an English Department Governance Committee (1985), appointed by Sutherland to restructure the department and move it out of receivership, offers a recommendation that, by its own admission, enhances the authority of the chair and tenured faculty. It also eliminates the troublesome Faculty Senate. James Sledd (1985) describes the "scheme" as "organized indecency." Then, on February 15, 1985, Sutherland announces to the department what has already been reported in the student newspaper: that the E 346K course requirement has been waived for the current year by a university vice president, and the course has been suspended, pending a departmental review. In his memo, Sutherland (1985a) notes that "the dean has recommended a Division of Composition," but Sutherland dismisses the possibility: "It seems irresponsible in the next difficult budget year to establish a new and costly administrative entity." However, with E346K canceled for fall 1985 (never to return), that budget will be lighter by the salaries of fifty-three lecturers to be axed after the spring term. So the WAC course is peremptorily gone, all but a handful of lecturers will soon depart, and a committee made up of (with one exception) professors of literature will restructure the entire composition program. As Maxine will observe just a few days later in Minneapolis, "for the literary establishment, the issue is power" (Hairston 1985, 274). It certainly was at Texas.

The gloves come in early March, at the next meeting of the Faculty Senate, with Kinneavy (1987b, 2127) submitting for the record a document titled "The Decomposition of English," describing the writing program as being "systematically dismantled"; Professor Sutherland (1985b) acknowledges at the meeting that, between factions in the English department, "there is very little kind of conversation back and forth." Predictably, the cancellation of E346K and the termination of the lecturers move the controversy into the public arena, with significant coverage in the student paper the *Daily Texan*, as well as the *Austin American-Statesman*, and eventually the *Chronicle of Higher Education*.

Combat by letters to the editor intensifies, especially after E 346K proponents James Kinneavy (1985a) and lecturer James Skaggs (1985) publish separate guest columns in the *Daily Texan* on February 20. Professor Larry Carver (1985), for example, responds with a piece assailing Kinneavy, lamenting that "rhetoricians . . . from the days of Socrates on down have never been much concerned with the truth." When another faculty member's reply to the Kinneavy/Skaggs columns is not published (possibly because the letter runs four pages), he shares his dittoed opinions with colleagues through faculty mailboxes. The date is March 4, and the author is once again Charles Rossman, the professor who, four years earlier, had imagined God and Satan debating the merit of composition programs. His arguments against rhetoric are familiar, but early in the letter, there is a fascinating detail: Rossman (1985) accuses Kinneavy and Skaggs of "depicting their opponents in the department as a cabal of self-serving mandarins who inexplicably stand in their way." Neither Kinneavy nor Skaggs uses the term *mandarin* in his column. But the word is clearly in circulation. By this point, I've seen a draft of Maxine's speech, and others may have as well.

This, then, is the atmosphere Maxine breathed as she prepared for her 4Cs address, delivered on March 21, 1985. Discourse in Austin may have been copious and fervent that spring term, but there hadn't been a rhetorical situation or persuadable audiences in the Department of English for many semesters. A closed fist of administrative fiat is displacing an open hand that, five years earlier, had welcomed a program designed, perhaps too ambitiously, to improve writing instruction. So, with "Breaking Our Bonds," Maxine takes a proposition always on the periphery of the debate, and moves it toward the center, the option she calls "the best one"—separation. How could she not?

Texts produced throughout the lengthy 346K/lecturer controversy—only a very few of which I've discussed here—were usually sincere, often long-winded, and occasionally clever. But only "Breaking Our Bonds" transcends its time. As chair of the 4Cs, Maxine seizes a rhetorical opportunity for which her experiences in Austin had prepared her perfectly. With a national audience of colleagues willing to be persuaded, she gives powerful expression to "a problem that requires attention right now," as Jimmie Killingsworth (2005, 27) glosses Bitzer's notion of exigence. At that moment, Hairston defines the issue of separation for a full generation of writing teachers and the independent writing programs *some* would build.

NOTE

Portions of this chapter were previously published: Ruszkiewicz, John. 2016. "Documents of Dissent: Hairston's 'Breaking Our Bonds' in Context." *College Composition and Communication* 68 (1), ed. Elizabeth Kalbfleisch, 179–85.

REFERENCES

Carver, Larry. 1985. "Literature, Composition Can Be Taught in the Same Class." *Daily Texan*, February 25, 3.

English Department Governance Committee. 1985. Memo to Tenured and Tenure-Track Faculty. February 11.

Hairston, Maxine. 1985. "Breaking Our Bonds and Reaffirming Our Connections." *College Composition and Communication* 36 (3): 272–82.

Heller, Scott. 1985. "50 Lecturers Lose Their Jobs in a Dispute over How—and If—Writing Can Be Taught." *Chronicle of Higher Education* (April 17): 23–24.

Killingsworth, M. Jimmie. 2005. *Appeals in Modern Rhetoric: An Ordinary-Language Approach*. Carbondale: Southern Illinois University Press.

King, Robert D. 1984. Letter to William Sutherland. September 14.

Kinneavy, James. 1984. "The Lecturers: Victims of Both Systems." Statement. March 26.

Kinneavy, James. 1985a. "Course Suspension Weakens Troubled Writing Program." *Daily Texan*, February 20, 2.

Kinneavy, James. 1985b. "The Decomposition of Composition." Minutes of the Faculty Senate, 2127. University of Texas at Austin, March 4.

Minutes of the Departmental Meeting. 1984. Department of English. University of Texas at Austin, April 19.

Moldenhauer, Joseph. 1980. Department of English Minutes. May 5.

Rossman, Charles. 1980. "'Position Paper' for Freshman Composition Committee—Format I." Department of English. University of Texas at Austin.

Rossman, Charles. 1985. "Misconceptions about the English 'Writing Program.'" Memo to English faculty. March 4.

Skaggs, James. 1985. "English Lecturers Deserve Better Treatment." *Daily Texan*, February 20, 2.

Sledd, James. 1982a. Documents and Proceedings of the University Council, 871–74. University of Texas at Austin, October 9.

Sledd, James. 1982b. "Misleading Statements by the English Department about Its New Requirements." Statement to Members of the University Council. University of Texas at Austin, December 7.

Sledd, James. 1985. "Tale of the 14 Stooges." *Daily Texan*, February 18.

Sutherland, W.O.S. 1985a. Memo to Members of the Department of English. University of Texas at Austin, February 15.

Sutherland, W.O.S. 1985b. Minutes of the Faculty Senate, 2130. University of Texas at Austin, March 4.

PART I

Adding Writing Majors or Minors during the Great Recession

2

FORGING INDEPENDENCE AND INNOVATION IN THE MIDST OF FINANCIAL AUSTERITY
The Syracuse University Writing Program

Lois Agnew and Eileen E. Schell

On June 2, 2016, the Syracuse Writing Program was granted permission to change its name to the Department of Writing Studies, Rhetoric and Composition. This name change was more symbolic than material. The Writing Program had been established as an independent academic unit almost thirty years previously, and it had functioned as a department with faculty tenure lines since the establishment of the PhD in composition and cultural rhetoric in 1997.

However, rhetoricians understand the importance of symbols, and the formal recognition of our departmental status is an important moment in a story that began in 1986, when the Writing Program split from the Department of English to form a separate academic unit. Prior to that time, the lower-division writing curriculum consisted of two courses, English 101 and 102, which were taught in six-week modules according to the Baker Essay Model. (An account of that curriculum can be found in several documents, including one written by WPA-consultant evaluators Donald McQuade and James Slevin [1984] and also Laura Davies's [2012] thoughtful dissertation detailing the history of the SU Writing Program during the period 1986–96.) If students were unable to pass the first module, they were channeled to part-time instructors who tutored them until they passed. Once that task was complete, students undertook the task of writing literary analysis essays focused on pieces of fiction and poetry.

Managed by Randall Brune, the freshman English program was geographically isolated from the rest of the English department. While the English department was located in the castle-like Hall of Languages, the teaching assistants (TAs) and part-time instructors who provided the bulk of freshman English instruction and tutoring were located in

DOI: 10.7330/9781607328957.c002

the basement of H. B. Crouse Hall, a modest brick structure located immediately behind the Hall of Languages. In the fall of 1983, thirty-nine teaching assistants and forty part-time faculty plus twelve part-time tutors, who provided 300 hours of tutoring per week, were responsible for the instruction in 168 sections of English 101 (Davies 2012, 13–14). Of the faculty housed in the English department, only two, Margaret Himley and Carol Lipson, taught or had training in writing and rhetoric.

With little or no faculty leadership, and a curriculum that was seriously out of step with the theories of writing and rhetoric prevailing in the 1980s, there was consensus that the freshman English model was not successful. In fact, so many complaints surfaced about the freshman English program that the University Senate took up the issue in a year-long program assessment led by Professor Bob Gates of the English department. Two visits by WPA consultant evaluators Donald McQuade and James Slevin took place in September and October 1984. The report from the Gates committee diagnosed a raft of problems: lack of investment of full-time English faculty in the program, a restrictive and unimaginative curriculum not in keeping with current theories in writing and rhetoric, a lack of professional development opportunities for part-time instructors, poor working conditions, and inadequate salaries. The Gates report, delivered to the University Senate in April 1985, made a series of recommendations, including a four-course writing sequence spread over the four years of the undergraduate experience, the hiring of a tenure-track writing program administrator to oversee the program, and improvement of the professional conditions of part-time instructors. The report also recommended that the writing program administrator should report to the dean of the College of Arts and Sciences, not the English department chair. Although the report did not explicitly recommend that the English department and the Writing Program should undergo a "divorce" along the lines Maxine Hairston trumpeted in her Conference on College Composition and Communication (CCCC) chair's address "Breaking Our Bonds and Reaffirming Our Connections" (cited in Davies 2012, 14–15), the suggestion that the Writing Program administrator would report directly to the dean served as the first step in a long process that led to the separation of the Writing Program and the English department.

Subsequent steps furthered the gradual division between the two units. The arrival of founding director Louise Phelps set the stage for the Writing Program's development as an independent academic unit, along with addressing many of the above-mentioned problems. The lower-division curriculum was revised and updated through the efforts of teams of part-time instructors, who were given long-term contracts with 3–2 loads and benefits that included healthcare, tuition benefits, and a retirement plan. As Laura Davies (2012, 79) puts it in her historical study of the first ten years of the SU Writing Program, "The full-time faculty members in the Writing Program needed the part-time instructors in order to create a viable program: the instructors knew the local Syracuse context and Syracuse students, and they were the ones who would interpret the new writing curriculum in their classrooms." Davies notes that professionalized part-time instructors who had access to professional development structures were key to the success of the program.

After receiving our charter as an independent unit in 1987, the 1997 establishment of the doctoral program in composition and cultural rhetoric served as an important next step toward operating as a fully functioning department. Before that time, faculty members from English with expertise in writing and rhetoric were jointly appointed in English and writing; with the addition of the doctoral program, those appointments were housed exclusively in writing. In 1999–2000, we underwent an expansion of the upper-division curriculum. Soon after, we also launched a series of service-learning writing courses that fostered engagement in community literacy and writing. Our writing minor was created in 2004, and the major in writing and rhetoric was formally approved in 2009.

BENEFITS AND GROWTH IN AN INDEPENDENT WRITING PROGRAM

This brief overview of our history makes clear that the name change signifying our official status as a department came long after we had been fully functioning as an academic unit. The long and gradual development of the Writing Program as an independent program at Syracuse University—now renamed the Department of Writing Studies, Rhetoric and Composition—has allowed us to engage with questions that have historically vexed our field, including what knowledge we claim to possess, how our vision of the links among rhetoric, literacy, ethics, and citizenship challenges the formulaic skills-based approach that is valued in the neo-liberal university, and how our commitment to expertise and fair labor practices can be sustained in an environment that is increasingly shaped by austerity. On a practical level, independence makes the knowledge and values of our field more visible, supports the expectation that all programmatic resources will be devoted to the development of a writing curriculum, and yields a degree of collegiality that is fostered when department members are united in their commitment to student writing and research in writing studies. Independence also allowed us to grow a writing and rhetoric major and graduate program without facing internal resistance that we might face in an English department, where such disciplinary developments might be seen as encroachments, or threats to literary studies, rather than opportunities to advance knowledge in writing and rhetoric.

The writing and rhetoric major, which started in 2007, is demonstrative of the program's ongoing commitment to strategic growth. When the program started in 1986, a spiral curriculum of four courses—WRT 105 (introduction to writing), WRT 205 (writing and research), WRT 305 (junior-level essay/inquiry), and WRT 405 (professional writing)—were the focal point of the curriculum. In 1999, under Louise Phelps's direction, the department expanded the two upper-division courses into eight courses that encompassed areas such as composition theory, creative nonfiction, literacy studies, digital writing, and rhetoric courses that examine topics in identity, technology, and culture. After starting a successful writing minor in 2004, and adding additional courses in language politics, style, and internships, we established a major in 2007. Since 2007, we have graduated over 150 students with a BA in writing and rhetoric, and we have a thriving community of undergraduate majors and alumni with impressive employment prospects.

A key component of our success and national reputation has been our innovative graduate program, which has attracted faculty and graduate students from across the country who wish to focus on studying, researching, and teaching writing and rhetoric. The idea of a doctoral program was present when the Writing Program began; the fifty-page proposal that developed over the next decade included two areas of focus: (1) composition studies, which built on the key insights of the field in relation to teaching and studying writing; and (2) cultural rhetoric, which addressed rhetoric as a historically and culturally situated practice and as a term open to inquiry and definition. The initial doctoral proposal failed to pass in the College of Arts and Sciences, but the subsequent proposal—which included consultation with many other units across campus—passed, and the program began in fall 1997.

Starting the doctoral program from scratch in the late 1990s was a major challenge. The entire infrastructure of the PhD had to be built with a handful of faculty members who were balancing responsibilities for the undergraduate program. Graduate courses had to be taught and revised, colloquia had to be scheduled, exam and dissertation processes had to be defined and codified, and professionalization events (such as job search processes) had to be specified. The work paid off over the years, as the program built from an initial three students to its current size of thirty or more students working on PhDs. Currently, we have granted over fifty PhDs; many of those graduates are tenured faculty members who are leaders in the field.

Even with these strategic areas of growth, independent writing programs are by no means immune to the well-known truth in our field that extraordinary service does not always lead to respect and appreciation. Although individual faculty members in our department have always been highly respected on campus, this view has not been consistently reflected in a broader appreciation of the academic vitality and curricular impact of our program.

ONGOING CHALLENGES IN INDEPENDENT WRITING PROGRAMS

Perhaps the most obvious challenge we have faced relates to the pressures our departmental responsibilities place on our teaching population. At Syracuse, the two-course introductory writing sequence required of all students entails approximately 250 sections per year. It is reasonable that an institution such as ours would balk at staffing this number of sections with research faculty on a 2–2 teaching load. Thanks to the vision of the faculty members who founded our program, the valuable contribution of part-time instructors (known as professional writing instructors, or PWIs) to our program's work has been materially acknowledged through multi-year contracts and benefits; this has resulted in a fairly stable teaching community in which diverse constituents can see that their work is important to the broader goals of the program. These part-time instructors were key—and still are—to building and teaching the undergraduate writing curriculum. Full-time instructorships were planned for as well but were not actually allowed until 2015. Having a thriving and active teaching community—whether part-time or full-time instructors—engaged in curricular change and innovation was central to the flourishing of the program as an independent unit.

At the same time our program was growing, the tenure system was gradually shrinking across disciplines nationally, which means that our tenure lines have not consistently increased with the program's expansion. These issues were particularly pronounced in the early 1990s, when the university experienced financial problems that led to a significant downsizing, and again in 2008, when the national recession led to hiring and pay freezes. Such moments have heightened a persistent pattern in which the university's reliance on our department to provide quality writing instruction to thousands of students has not always been accompanied by the resources necessary to carry out our mission. This has resulted in a department that has been consistently stretched to the limit. Our tenure-track faculty have barely been able to cover the responsibilities that have come with the department's growth, including supervision of lower-division teaching and curriculum, TA education, the major/minor, community literacy initiatives, and the graduate program. In a traditional English department, such work would be undertaken by twenty–forty tenure-line faculty members; in our department, approximately ten faculty members take up this work. Faculty members in our department have also consistently faced the challenges of fostering coherence and community across a large and diverse teaching population and aligning our curriculum with current research in our field while showing respect for the practical experience of our PWIs. At the same time, they have navigated the challenge of balancing the goals of research, teaching, and service in a department that requires a higher volume of administrative work than that found in many academic departments.

The department's extensive reach across campus also entails the expectation that we will be responsive to changes in the university. While all faculty are affected, to some extent, by new leadership and changing student populations, our dynamic relationship with students and the acknowledged importance of writing among faculty across campus place our department's work under particular scrutiny. Most writing programs deal with complaints about the quality of student writing and the implicit blame that is associated with those complaints. As an independent writing program at a private, tuition-driven university, we know that these concerns reflect profound philosophical differences concerning the nature of literacy, the purpose of rhetorical education, and the relationship between rhetoric and citizenship.

As with all aspects of our work, local conditions play a major role in how these conversations play out. Syracuse University's history includes a strong commitment to the liberal arts, which over time has been complemented by the development of prestigious and highly ranked professional schools. The strength of professional education at Syracuse, coupled with a national landscape in which educational values are often driven by the immediate career benefits available to students, imposes particular pressures on an academic unit whose work is seen as "serving" students across the university. A further complication is that colleagues across the university find it difficult to understand our discipline's unique integration of theory with practice. Our department often faces questions from all sides: for our colleagues in the College of Arts and Sciences, our work may appear to be insufficiently theoretical, while faculty members in the professional schools may express bafflement over our determination to complicate what to them should be easily taught practical skills in the required writing courses. Moreover, the responsibilities for writing instruction are distributed among multiple stakeholders at Syracuse who have varied ways of understanding what "good writing" looks like, articulating the goals of writing courses, and defining the pedagogical methods that will best achieve those goals. While the university's tendency to create silos of expertise that operate somewhat independently of each other has yielded benefits in fostering excellence and innovation within individual academic units, it has also had the less positive outcome of establishing competing perspectives about literacy that could be usefully nuanced through greater communication and collaboration across departments and schools and colleges.

In addition to the challenges that may have been exacerbated by independence, our academic unit has received a number of benefits that would not have been available if our department were less visible on campus. In addition to the pressure of responding to changing academic environments, we have played an important role in developing key initiatives on campus. The university's emphases on research and teaching, diversity, internationalization, community engagement, innovative pedagogies, and veterans' concerns have allowed us to find meaningful connections between our work and the varied priorities the university has adopted in recent years. There are times when our ideas about the purpose and scope of these initiatives have not been precisely aligned with the vision of others on campus, and the task of negotiating across such differences is a key feature of our work.

One recent development illustrates the types of ongoing opportunities and challenges involved in sustaining a large and dynamic department in a changing academic environment. For many years, a pattern of enrollment growth alongside stagnation in tenure-track hiring approvals had led to a rapid increase in the number of part-time instructors in our department. In 2015, our recently appointed dean authorized us to hire full-time non-tenure-track instructors to help cover the growth in introductory writing sections and create further stability in our teaching community; the majority of instructors hired that year were longtime PWIs who were given the opportunity of full-time employment after many years of excellent part-time teaching in our program. This change has required that we work through the practical details surrounding Michael Murphy's (2000, 25) notion of "career-track instructorships" who are "recognized as legitimate full-time academic citizens with governance responsibilities and salaries running parallel to, although somewhat behind, that of traditional faculty." These details include determining the role of non-tenure-track instructors in governance, meeting the department's service needs without overloading instructors in teaching-intensive positions, and developing structures for evaluating and promoting these faculty members. Meanwhile, conversations about these positions with colleagues across the university have repeatedly touched on the question of whether pursuing full-time non-tenure-track appointments is complicit in the erosion of the tenure system that has been one outcome of the corporate university. While we advocate for the tenure system at every possible opportunity, our disciplinary location requires that we balance this ideal against the need to be constantly attentive to the working conditions of our instructors, along with recognizing ways student learning is enhanced through providing more faculty members with opportunities to be on our campus full-time rather than cobbling together a livable salary by teaching at multiple institutions. This is just one example of the complex and evolving network of material and ethical concerns that surround the work of the independent writing program.

The changes that have taken place in our department over time reflect the persistent interactions among departmental goals and institutional constraints. Part of the success of the Syracuse experiment has been consistently to build intellectual community, encourage curricular experimentation, and work toward programmatic goals incrementally over time. This enterprise has required that we continually respond to the challenges we face as an independent writing program—including responding to the expectations of external stakeholders, managing financial constraints, and maintaining ethical labor practices—while tenaciously advancing our own vision of becoming a fully functioning academic department that focuses on writing and rhetoric research and teaching at every level. While our departmental life is not idyllic, we celebrate the progress we have made in achieving the goals that were established for our program thirty years ago. Certainly, the vibrant and intellectually engaged students and faculty who inhabit the Department of Writing Studies, Rhetoric and Composition today are in a much better place than those who operated the freshman English program of the early 1980s from the physical and intellectual isolation of the H. B. Crouse Hall basement.

REFLECTION

The postscript poses a number of questions that usefully illuminate major themes that define the story of the Syracuse Writing Program. Although it is tempting to see our highly publicized "divorce" from the English department as the defining moment in our program's history, this event in fact only functioned to create the space needed to make possible the developments that have truly defined our department: the cultivation of a vibrant and dynamic introductory writing program, the PhD program in composition and cultural rhetoric, the writing minor, the writing and rhetoric major, and connected community engagement projects. We have definitely moved beyond the divorce narrative.

These developments and collaborations have consistently engaged us in defining disciplinary expertise that is interdisciplinary in nature. The varied understandings of writing and literacy on our campus have required us to assert a disciplinary perspective that differs substantially from others. Our ability to argue successfully for a doctoral program, minor, and major, has required us to define the parameters of our offerings while assuring our colleagues that we offer unique expertise that cannot be found elsewhere on campus. At the same time, the vitality of our program has depended upon our awareness of the intrinsic interdisciplinarity of writing and rhetoric scholarship and pedagogy. Although we should be cautious about measures that blur disciplinary boundaries to support austerity measures, our department's history reveals the value of dialogue and action that has enabled us to share our expertise and to collaborate successfully with colleagues across disciplines.

NOTE

Portions of this chapter were previously published: Agnew, Lois, and Eileen E. Schell. 2016. "Forging Independence and Innovation in the Midst of Financial Austerity: The Syracuse University Writing Program." *College Composition and Communication* 68 (1), ed. Elizabeth Kalbfleisch, 191–95.

REFERENCES

Davies, Laura. 2012. "Lightning in a Bottle: A History of the Syracuse Writing Program, 1986–1996." PhD dissertation, Syracuse University, Syracuse, NY.

McQuade, Donald A., and James A. Slevin. 1984. "Council of Writing Program Administrators Evaluation Report, Syracuse University, September 27–28, November 8–9, 1984."

Murphy, Michael. 2000. "New Faculty for a New University: Toward a Full-Time Teaching Intensive Faculty Track in Composition." *College Composition and Communication* 52 (1): 14–42.

"Syracuse University Proposal for PhD in Composition and Cultural Rhetoric." 1996. The Writing Program, Syracuse University, Syracuse, NY.

3

FORCES ACTING ON A DEPARTMENTAL (RE-)MERGER
Budgets, Spaces, Disciplines, Identities

David Beard and Chongwon Park

This chapter discusses the struggle of an independent writing program and an independent linguistics program; both were required to merge with a Department of English after more than twenty years of autonomy. This chapter works in four steps.

- First, it maps the growth of the autonomous Department of Writing Studies at the University of Minnesota Duluth (UMD). Our success was one of the reasons we are being merged with English—the merger promises a revived environment for English at UMD.

- Second, it looks at some of the problems the merger was to solve: problems of budget and of space. We talk about the relative effectiveness of the merger as a solution to those problems.

- Third, it looks at problems the merger created and the attempts to address those problems. Largely, these included problems of governance.

- We conclude by describing the tensions in the merger process, tensions rooted in disciplinarity and identity.

Relative to our first account of the merger (Beard and Park 2016), we are more worn, more exhausted, by what this process has demanded of us and our colleagues. Our insights may be useful to others, but we also write to argue that our experiences here contribute to research in the sociology of disciplines. As David Shumway and Ellen Messer-Davidow (1991, 208, quoting Geiger 1986) note, a discipline is a "community based on inquiry and centered on competent investigators. It consists of individuals who associated in order to facilitate intercommunication and to establish some degree of authority over the standards of that inquiry." The re-merger of English (literature) faculty with linguistics and writing studies faculty tests the relationship between disciplines and departments, between an identity as a scholar in the community of a

DOI: 10.7330/9781607328957.c003

discipline and as a member in the community of a department, in ways that may be valuable to other departments in a time of austerity.

HISTORICAL CONTEXT FOR THE DEPARTMENT OF WRITING STUDIES AT THE UNIVERSITY OF MINNESOTA DULUTH

Below, we survey the history of writing instruction at UMD in the journalism curriculum, the linguistics curriculum, and the professional and first-year writing curricula. This history illustrates our claim that for the bulk of the twentieth century at UMD, the history of writing enacted what James Berlin (1987) called the split between production and consumption in academic life.

In the 1960s, interest in courses in propaganda, journalism, and media writing rose; the collection of those courses became a "communications" program housed in English. In the 1970s, the "communications" program moved to the newly named Department of Speech Communication. There, it was segregated from the "speech communication" curriculum in the way courses in production are often segregated from courses in criticism. To emphasize the split between production and consumption, "communications" was renamed "journalism." (Quickly finishing the story of journalism at UMD: the journalism program moved again to the Department of Composition in the 1990s, housing all courses in the production of writing. The journalism program rejoined communication in 2017.)

The Department of Composition was formed in 1987, when the faculty in the then–Department of English agreed to divide into two departments—one for the delivery of the literature major and one for the delivery of writing courses. The linguistics faculty joined the composition department in the hope that the skills achieved through linguistics would enhance students' writing ability. The split was amicable; literature faculty were grateful that literature courses would no longer compete with writing courses for budget dollars. Writing faculty (and the linguistics faculty who worked alongside them) preferred an institutional context of self-determination.

Between 1987 and 2013, the linguistics program grew rapidly, developing first an undergraduate minor, then a graduate minor. The program embedded itself in the university, teaching elective courses in the history of the English language for the literature program and courses in linguistic anthropology for the anthropology program. In 2014, a wholly independent BS in linguistics began to be offered. This new major places emphasis on the scientific nature of the discipline, and the aforementioned elective courses were removed from the core curriculum.

Summarizing the rise to autonomy of the Program in Writing Studies: after founding a department in 1987, the leaders in the Department of Composition began to think more entrepreneurially. They reclaimed journalism, eventually housing minors in journalism, linguistics, professional communication, and information design. They also developed graduate courses. By the early 2000s, the Department of Composition was home to four minors, graduate coursework, and two university-wide writing course requirements. The department had become home to multiple forms of writing production (whether in academic, professional, or mass communication contexts) and both the rhetorical and the scientific study of language. By 2009, the time was ripe to synthesize that coursework into a major in writing studies (discussed in Beard 2010a, 2010b).

CURRICULAR STRUCTURE FOR A MAJOR IN WRITING STUDIES AT THE UNIVERSITY OF MINNESOTA DULUTH

In 2009, when we debuted the major in writing studies (and changed our name to the Department of Writing Studies), we did so echoing two larger shifts:

- The move to rethink our work from "composition" (signaling first-year writing to many) toward a larger disciplinary project, and
- The move on the Twin Cities campus to create a new department emphasizing writing instruction, also called the Department of Writing Studies.

The term was drawn from Charles Bazerman ("The Case for Writing Studies as a Major Field of Study"). Therein, Bazerman (2002, 32) claims that "Writing Studies is the study of writing—its production, its circulation, its uses, its role in the development of individuals, societies and cultures." The major includes coursework in these areas: required courses in the history of literacy, in media law and ethics, and in new media writing.

Because of our unique, twenty-year collaboration with the faculty in linguistics, and because Bazerman's definition opens us to cognitive understandings of the work of writing, we initially integrated linguistics into the curriculum. The writing studies major included one linguistics course in its core courses. The course was designed to help students discover the descriptive grammar they already use unconsciously. This course was removed from the core when the program was reevaluated in fall 2013. This is not because the descriptive grammar is unimportant but because it is less tightly connected to the writing studies major in the sense that the grammar deals with both spoken and written forms, while analyzing spoken forms of language plays a less important role in writing.

The major initially included emphases in journalism (discontinued in 2017) and in professional writing corresponding to the minors that contributed coursework to the major. Enrollment in the major did not cannibalize enrollment in the minors; rather, the rising tide lifted all boats.

We draw students who value the ability to produce and not only critique texts, videos, websites, and new media projects. We serve as a complementary program for liberal arts programs, from English and communication, to history and sociology. We have been a success, and our success is one rationale for our merger with the Department of English.

HISTORICAL CONTEXT FOR A RE-MERGER WITH ENGLISH

To understand why the administration desires a re-merger of the faculty in writing studies with English, we note the state of enrollments in English. English exists in a more vigorous, more competitive university environment. Its share of the "pie" of university enrollments is declining. Nationally, we have moved from a period in which one in eight undergraduates was an English major, to a context in which one in twenty-five undergraduates is an English major (Schramm et al. 2003). Nationally, there is a squirming anxiety that literary studies may go the way of the Classics. As Victor Davis Hanson and John Heath tell us in *Who Killed Homer* (2001), enrollment in the Classics dropped 30 percent between 1971 and 1991 and never recovered. Enrollments in English have declined at UMD in recent years; we are not bucking national trends.

The English department at UMD has streamlined its curriculum and is working to develop a new major in creative writing to draw more students. Meanwhile, nationwide, the number of writing majors is growing: "In our first investigation (2005), we found 45 institutions that offered majors in rhetoric and composition; as of this writing (2008), the number stands at 68 in 65 different institutions . . . [A] significant amount of institutional change is underway. Although we have just four years' worth of data, it does seem that the major is growing at an impressive rate" (Balzhiser and McLeod 2010, 416). UMD's writing studies major is small—about two dozen students—but it participates in such growth. A merger may stabilize enrollments in both programs.

Wrapped into this national climate of change is the merger of English and writing studies.

MERGER AS A RESPONSE TO PROBLEMS: BUDGETS AND SPACE

The UMD administration has used the merger to respond to two ongoing problems at the university: (1) a budgetary shortfall caused by underfunding from the state and a dip in enrollment and (2) space needs.

The merger responds to budgetary problems at UMD: a $6 million structural deficit. As a result, in fall 2014, every academic program was subject to "program prioritization," a process adapted from the systems mapped in Robert C. Dickeson's *Prioritizing Academic Programs and Services: Reallocating Resources to Achieve Strategic Balance.* In that process, a number of university offices were closed, a minor in cultural studies was shuttered, and at a more local level, the Department of Writing Studies lost a three-quarter-time administrative assistant.

Further budget cuts followed, resulting in the loss of adjunct faculty members (three in the Writing Studies Program) and a push to combine departments across the College of Liberal Arts. Small savings would follow from reducing the total number of course releases given to department heads, reducing the number of summer supplements for administrative work given to department heads, and reducing the number of support staff. We were the first department to be merged, but we would not be the last.

We should put the budget savings into small perspective. Four non-major service writing courses were assigned to English faculty, thereby leading to the cut of the same number of English courses. This type of course reassignment was the first time in a decade such assignments had been made, at a rough savings of ($6,000 per section) × (4 sections), for a baseline of $24,000. In addition, three course releases were saved (as the merged department has only one head), for a baseline of $18,000. Also, a summer supplement of $6,000 was saved. In total, the equivalent of one non-tenure-track faculty member's salary was saved ($48,000); the benefits package adds another $20,000 in savings, for a total savings of about $68,000. If administration acts aggressively (cancelling more low-enrollment sections of literature courses, which are capped at fifteen students, and replacing them with writing classes capped at twenty-five), we could see this savings increase.

The merger was already justification for losing a three-quarter-time administrative assistant (a nine-month position, including benefits) and several adjunct faculty. Merging departments, then, has been a substantive response to budgetary shortfalls at UMD, gains mostly made possible (as is often the case at the university) by losing support staff and adjunct faculty.

A second ongoing pressure on the university has been an increase in space needs. The program in writing studies offers more and more classes, for example, online and night classes, to accommodate increasing pressure on classroom space. But, with the increasing number of administrative staff at the university, there are increasing pressures on office space. Faculty members are perceived as inefficient users of space, occupying their offices for fewer than forty hours a week, while administrative staff (in, for example, advising, promotions, development) occupy their offices for forty hours weekly. The merger of the two departments created an opportunity to respond to these space pressures.

As two departments, both English and writing studies maintained reception spaces. A merged department does not need two suites for support staff. More than $200,000 was allocated to remodel the suites to accommodate workstations (single-seat cubicles) for fourteen adjunct faculty members, with a "FERPA room" for faculty to sign out when meeting with students. While administration remained committed to the quality of the workstations, the writing program administrator and tenured faculty in the writing program objected, noting that if each writing instructor scheduled one twenty-minute conference with each student each semester, the FERPA room would be "checked out" for 350 hours. (The preferred pedagogy for the course includes three conferences, or more than a thousand hours of individual conferencing.) The administrative plan, in other words, did not provide adequate office space for best practices in writing pedagogy.

Administration returned with a redesign—larger cubicles for eight adjunct faculty. While the writing program faculty continued to oppose the office redesign plan, the mechanisms for refusal were becoming limited. Members of the department went to our union (UEA-D), which referenced the line in the contract arguing that all members (tenure track and non-tenure track) will be given "comparable" office space. No other unit on campus attempted to put fourteen or even eight faculty in a single room, no matter how nice the cubicles are. Threatening to grieve the proposed change, the *union* secured from the dean's office what the *department* could not—the administration backed down from the proposed change.

The union collected data on comparable office spaces. Of the twenty-eight shared faculty office spaces on the entire campus, across five colleges, the union noted that sixteen were in the College of Liberal Arts (while twelve were in the four remaining colleges total), and the union has partnered with administration to rectify this imbalance.

MERGER CREATES PROBLEMS: GOVERNANCE

In the first year of the merger (2016–17), the department operated as a kind of "two-headed hydra," with two department heads. In many ways, the departments continued to act largely autonomously during this year, meeting by program to discuss curriculum, for example, instead of meeting as a department. While this structure moved forward, the work of a merger committee continued in a new form.

For the two years prior to merger, a joint committee of faculty met in a mixed process that, at different points, led to suggestions everywhere from a full merger (with a single major) to proposing merging with different departments (English with foreign languages and literatures, writing studies with communication, and linguistics with philosophy). The committee looked to peer institutions, to statements from professional associations, and to other merged departments at UMD for guidance. We worked with an external consultant, a specialist in navigating organizational change, although that process did not win a buy-in from faculty in both departments.

In our initial merger meetings, we focused on procedural questions:

- Merging our tenure and promotion statements
- Establishing our constitution and bylaws, as neither department had them previously
- As significant subtasks within the constitution and bylaws, we also began work in
- Establishing criteria for departmental membership
- Establishing participation and processes for committee membership
- Establishing scheduling procedures and curricular authority
- Establishing processes for departmental elections

The details of each of these tasks are explained below.

We began the process of creating a single *tenure and promotion statement* for the merged department. Because a significant portion of the document is determined by a university boilerplate, we found ourselves arguing over small segments. The document, for example, was to have a "mission" statement, and we discussed whether we had one unified mission or one mission to offer three programs (English, linguistics, and writing studies). These discussions were not simple, but generally, when the genre is tightly circumscribed, the collaboration is easy.

A *constitution and bylaws* became more vexing, so a committee member found a precedent for creating a document called "operating procedures," which seemed to offer lower stakes, though it would serve the same functions as a constitution and bylaws.

Membership. Within English, a small department of fewer than twelve faculty and few adjunct faculty (often sabbatical replacements, sometimes spousal hires, always with full-time appointments), membership was crisp and clear: full membership and rights were given to tenure-line faculty. Within writing studies, membership was complicated by the diversity of appointments. We employed faculty with part-time or split appointments with other units, for example. And in a stronger contrast with English, all faculty, tenure-track or non-tenure-track, were fully vested members with rights in all areas of the department (other than personnel decisions).

Merging these two standards for membership in the department was difficult. Luckily, we could point to a College Constitution that defined membership in the college (and therefore eligibility for voting and service in college-wide issues) at a 65 percent appointment in the current year. Arguing that we could not reasonably expect our faculty to serve on college committees and vote on college issues while unable to do the same within the department, we established the college's definitions of membership as the baseline for future membership in the merged department.

Participation in Committees

That said, participation in committees in the Department of Writing Studies was set by policy; under those policies, non-tenure-track faculty were defined into roles within departmental committees. This was a gesture of egalitarianism as well as efficiency—a committee to work on assessment of writing courses, for example, built without the participation and leadership of the faculty who teach 90 percent of those courses would be doing futile work. Our non-tenure-track (NTT) colleagues are our collaborators. There were no similar policies in place in English (and at moments, there was friction over NTT participation in the merger committees). In the revised operating procedures, only the committee overseeing the first-year writing and other service writing courses included defined, required participation by NTT faculty. Individual committee chairs could invite NTT participation as they desired. (The norms of English, in other words, were upheld.)

Scheduling and Curriculum

Following the model of sociology, anthropology, and criminology (three majors within one merged department at UMD), we established curricular autonomy across writing studies, linguistics, and English. That curricular autonomy was tested when the administration announced that twenty-one sections of non-major service writing courses would go unfunded (and the NTT faculty who taught them would not be renewed), and that the department would need to find some solutions. We eliminated several electives in the writing studies major and minors, adding a section of first-year writing to each tenure-line faculty member's schedule. We cut partially enrolled sections and replaced them with more-likely-to-fill online sections. We pulled writing studies faculty who had been released to teach in other units (courses in photojournalism, for example, or world religions in the philosophy program) back to teach in writing studies. And we were still short.

Arguments about curricular autonomy and independence of programs were not persuasive in a context of budgetary constraint. English faculty were asked to teach sections of non-major, service first-year and upper-division writing courses to make up the shortfall (as noted above, they picked up four sections). It's unclear what ramifications this will have for long-term collegiality between WRIT and ENGL faculty. No one in writing studies wanted to see our colleagues fired so their classes could be assigned to people who would prefer not to teach them. No one in English sought to displace writing studies faculty or to teach these classes. Budgetary constraints forced decisions no one wanted, ones no degree of departmental negotiation, as part of the merger, could stop.

Departmental Elections

All departments in our college are governed by a department head, recommended to the dean after a faculty election. Our two departments recommended faculty to the dean differently:

- Within the English department, there is an election, held only among the tenure-track members of the department, in which "the next most senior tenured faculty member who has not yet served as head" is typically recommended to the dean. This process means that nearly everyone in the department has served a three-year term as head. This creates a powerful problem-solving team. It also means that faculty with definite weaknesses as administrators are still asked to lead—something that seems functional in a very small department

but that (from the perspective of the authors) carries risk in a
department that is one-fifth the size of the entire college.

- Within the Department of Writing Studies, all faculty, including
  adjunct faculty, vote for the head in a genuine election that allows
  for reelection to multiple terms. Historically, this has caused its own
  problems, as several faculty have served for multiple terms (playing,
  perhaps, to those faculty members' strengths but also drawing them
  away from other strengths in research and teaching).

On the one hand, this appears to be a procedural difference—simply
a matter of hammering out bylaws. On the other hand, this procedural
difference reflects more profound cultural differences.

First, it reflects a tension in the different ways we conceive of leadership. Like the classical political figures who served their government
and then went back to their farms, the English faculty serve (sometimes
reluctantly, sometimes with enthusiasm) and return to their lives as
teachers and scholars. In writing studies, in contrast, administrative work
is more complicated. Our budget dwarfs the English budget, with more
than twenty adjunct faculty, eight graduate assistants, and eight tenure-
line faculty. Administration becomes a career path for some heads of
writing studies, as the leap from administering a fifth of the college to
full-time administration is small.

Since the first appearance of critical reflection on this process in college composition and communication (CCC), these tensions have wors-
ened. A probably overcomplicated election process for the next head,
which compromised both sides, went forward with full departmental
approval. That process was largely ignored as the ballot circulated asking
departmental members to identify their program and status as tenure
stream or non-tenure stream (reproducing, then, the basic processes
in English before the merger). Adjunct faculty felt vulnerable in that
election context, and tenure-line faculty in literature, then, could report
that they were united behind one candidate when results were reported
to the dean.

Complaints that this ballot was not in compliance with the operating procedures were greeted curtly. One individual noted that revising
the ballot to be in compliance with the operating procedures would
not change the outcome of the election. Disheartened, the writing
studies faculty member who raised the complaint (Beard) replied
that he didn't think we only followed the operating procedures when
following the rules would change the outcome of the election. And
so the ballot moved forward, out of compliance with the operating procedures.

RETHINKING THE RELATIONSHIP BETWEEN
DEPARTMENTS AND PROGRAMS

We'd like to gesture for a moment to the ways a recombined department becomes a site for reflection on the sociology of knowledge. As Shumway and Messer-Davidow (1991, 209) note, "The organizational structure of the research university developed so as to permit disciplinary practitioners to exercise . . . authority. Departments were in principle given control over hiring, tenure, and curriculum." This seems obvious—literature faculty should control hiring, tenure, and curriculum in literature. A merged department questions these practices. While we have tried to make curriculum autonomous, hiring and tenure are now departmental negotiations. Whether the next line will be in linguistics, writing studies, or English, will be subject to departmental discussion.

But, perhaps more significant, none of us shares intellectual associations beyond membership in this department. All of us share identities outside the university with "national and international institutions that embodied the disciplines-professional associations that sponsored disciplinary activities and promulgated disciplinary values, journals that published disciplinary and specialized research, funding agencies that supported disciplinary research and teaching, and peer reviewers who evaluated disciplinary work" (Shumway and Messer-Davidow 1991, 209). We imagine ourselves, in other words, to be three disciplines administered by one head.

The outside world is more likely to view us in the light of K–12 education, in which language, literature, and writing are one subject. We worry, as we move forward, that we will expend too much energy establishing our differences within the department, while our real energy should be spent on establishing our differences and our diverse values to those outside the department.

MOVING FORWARD CAREFULLY

The merger was completed superficially in 2016, but the division among the groups—linguistics, writing studies, and English—is still visible, and understanding each other's cultures remains on our "to-do" list.

We are doing our best to remain prominent in the minds of administration, students, and the public. We issue press releases regularly about our events and track media pickup. We prepare departmental newsletters promoting our work. We are establishing our value and our identity as programs in the university. Our independence as a writing program came because of our strength; we retain that strength even if we lose our independence.

REFLECTION

Regarding the introduction's postscript, we are asked to locate questions about the future of independent writing programs in terms of Allen Repko, Rich Szostak, and Michelle Phillips Buchberger's (2013) understandings of "multidisciplinarity" and "transdisciplinarity." This framework for understanding our work may resonate with some readers.

Neither multidisciplinarity nor interdisciplinarity resonates with our experience. Decades of autonomy as linguists and rhetoricians gave us a sense of disciplinarity. Tony Becher (1989, 33) argues that "knowledge communities are defined and reinforced by the 'nurturance of myth, the identification of unifying symbols, the canonization of exemplars, and the formation of guilds.'" In this way, the construction of a discipline is contrary to the work of today's university, which may require rethinking or challenging disciplinary myths and guilds. But disciplinarity comes with strengths; Julie Thompson Klein (1996, 46–48) provides us with terms to describe disciplines. Disciplines have

- *a material field*, a set of objects for study
- *theory and law*, the explanatory models validated in the research
- *methods* and *analytical tools*, including experimentation, statistics, criticism,
- and a *problem set.*

As disciplines of writing studies and linguistics, we bring refined sets of knowledge and practices to any collaboration. As we question the myths and guilds, we also value our theories and methods and what they bring to problems we might investigate with others.

While re-merger has been described as an opportunity to institutionalize interdisciplinarity, it has been experienced as an exercise of power. It manifested the power of the administration to realign budgets with enrollment by course reassignment. It has manifested the power of a subset of tenured faculty to force their norms and practices upon a merged department. And where we have succeeded in resisting the exercise of power, we have not done so as a discipline but as members of a union (in defeating the reassignment of fourteen adjuncts in one office). We happily pick up Repko, Szostak, and Phillips Buchberger, but we recommend that our colleagues also reread their Foucault.

NOTE

Portions of this chapter were previously published: Beard, David, and Chongwon Park. 2016. "In Medias Res: Sustaining a Program in Writing Studies in the Context of Department Merger." *College Composition and Communication* 68 (1), ed. Elizabeth Kalbfleisch, 196–200.

REFERENCES

Balzhiser, Deborah, and Susan H. McLeod. 2010. "The Undergraduate Writing Major: What Is It? What Should It Be?" *College Composition and Communication* 61 (3): 415–33.

Bazerman, Charles. 2002. "The Case for Writing Studies as a Major Field of Study." In *Rhetoric and Composition as Intellectual Work*, ed. Gary A. Olson, 32–38. Carbondale: Southern Illinois University Press.

Beard, David. 2010a. "The Case for a Major in Writing Studies: The University of Minnesota Duluth." *Composition Forum* 21. http://compositionforum.com/issue/21/minnesota-duluth.php.

Beard, David. 2010b. "Writing Studies as Grounds for Professional Writing: The Major at the University of Minnesota Duluth" *Programmatic Perspectives* 2 (2). http://www.cptsc.org/pp/vol2–2/beard2–2.pdf.

Beard, David, and Chongwon Park. 2016. "In Medias Res: Sustaining a Program in Writing Studies in the Context of Departmental Merger." In "CCC Symposia on IWP in the Post-Recessionary Era," ed. Elizabeth Kalbfleisch and Matthew Abraham. *College Composition and Communication* 68 (1): 196–99.

Becher, Tony. 1989. *Academic Tribes and Territories: Intellectual Inquiry and the Culture of Disciplines*. Stony Stratford, UK: Society for Research into Higher Education and Open University Press.

Berlin, James. 1987. *Rhetoric and Reality: Writing Instruction in American Colleges, 1900–1985*. Carbondale: Southern Illinois University Press.

Dickeson, Robert C. 2010. *Prioritizing Academic Programs and Services: Reallocating Resources to Achieve Strategic Balance*. San Francisco: Jossey-Bass.

Geiger, Roger L. 1986. *To Advance Knowledge: The Growth of American Research Universities, 1900–1940*. New York: Oxford University Press.

Hanson, Victor Davis, and John Heath. 2001. *Who Killed Homer? The Demise of Classical Education and the Recovery of Greek Wisdom*. San Francisco: Encounter Books.

Klein, Julie Thompson. 1996. *Crossing Boundaries*. Charlottesville: University Press of Virginia.

Repko, Allen, Rich Szostak, and Michelle Phillips Buchberger. 2013. *Introduction to Interdisciplinary Studies*. Thousand Oaks, CA: Sage.

Schramm, Margaret, J. Lawrence Mitchell, Delores Stephens, and David Laurence. 2003. "The Undergraduate English Major." *ADE Bulletin* 134–35: 68–91.

Shumway, David R., and Ellen Messer-Davidow. 1991. "Disciplinarity." *Poetics Today* 12 (2): 201–25.

4

GROWING DESPITE AUSTERITY
The Department of Rhetoric and Writing at the University of Texas at Austin

Mark Garrett Longaker, Davida Charney,
Diane Davis, and Alice Batt

Like many independent writing departments, we have faced recent challenges. In the fall of 2009, our lower-division budget was cut by nearly 40 percent. In the spring of 2013, the College of Liberal Arts suggested merging the administrative staff of the DRW with that of another (or several other) departments. And in the fall of 2014, a college-level committee proposed that the DRW merge with English and that we reduce the number of rhetoric and writing faculty by 36 percent. We have avoided such mergers and abated the effects of such financial cuts by expanding our mission. A brief history of the department and a survey of our four major units demonstrate this strategy of growth despite austerity.

On September 1, 1992, the University of Texas at Austin's Division of Rhetoric and Composition (DRC) was born of tensions between the English literature and the rhetoric and writing faculty. At its humble beginning, the DRC boasted six tenured or tenure-track faculty, two adjuncts, two centers (the Computer Writing and Research Lab and the Undergraduate Writing Center), and three courses (RHE 306: Rhetoric and Composition, RHE 309K: Topics in Writing, and RHE 325M: Advanced Writing). In time, the DRC faculty developed a series of upper-division courses, acquired new faculty lines, and eventually created a rhetoric and writing major. If we had remained a division overseeing one required writing class (RHE 306), we would have been folded back into English once faculty acrimony waned. Improving the core writing curriculum, adding a major, and expanding the centers has allowed the DRW to remain an autonomous department, despite UT Austin's efforts at consolidating, downsizing, and eliminating other small departments and programs.

DOI: 10.7330/9781607328957.c004

More important, though, expanding our mission has expanded the possibilities for rhetoric and writing. At its beginning, our discipline depended on a core course whose administration is always fraught and whose future is often uncertain. The required writing course was born in the early twentieth century amid concerns about student deficiency. It grew as enrollments ballooned. In recent decades, media have dramatically affected our composing habits, and writing in the disciplines programs have challenged the wisdom of the first-year course. Should we be teaching students to write academic papers when they'll collaboratively compose electronic and dynamic texts in their later classes and in their careers? Should we expect one class to inoculate students against poor writing when a steady diet of practice and disciplinary training works just as well, if not better? In the face of these challenges and concerns, amid difficult financial times, the DRW has chosen to invest in an expanded mission that serves the wider university by means other than the basic course. We preserve our commitment to RHE 306, as discussed below, but we look for other and more varied ways to promote writing (and rhetoric) at our university. This diversified approach has allowed our department to grow, even as other programs in the College of Liberal Arts downsize, shrink, or disappear. Our diversified approach has additionally expanded the discipline of rhetoric and writing to include new media (and the institutional support centers that research and develop such media), writing in the disciplines (including graduate-student writing), rhetoric (in all its forms), and professional writing (technical and otherwise).

THE CORE WRITING CURRICULUM

Transfer credit and credit by exam have reduced the number of students who take UT's required writing course (RHE 306) in residence. We now invest time and energy into a suite of elective lower-division "writing-flag" courses that fulfill university (not state) curricular requirements. We have developed fresh courses that interest undergraduates, with titles such as:

RHE 312: Writing in Digital Environments
RHE 315: Visual Rhetoric
RHE 309K: The Rhetoric of Video Games
RHE 309K: The Rhetoric of Harry Potter
RHE 309K: The Rhetoric of Satire

The 309K titles have been featured in the student newspaper and on the university homepage. Because these lower-division writing-flag courses are so popular, their enrollment often rivals that in RHE 306. For instance, in the 2015–16 academic year, 879 students enrolled in RHE 306 (across fifty sections) while 865 students enrolled in RHE 309K, RHE 309S, RHE 315, and RHE 312 (across thirty-seven sections combined). As enrollment in our required writing course (RHE 306) has shrunk, enrollment in our elective writing courses has grown. When we make our annual budgetary request to fund lower-division courses, we point to the long lines of waitlisted students wanting to take, for instance, the Rhetoric of Facebook or the Rhetoric of Action Films (both recent sections of RHE 309K). Our ability to enroll more students in elective lower-division writing classes, in fact, is hampered by our obligation to offer enough sections of RHE 306 to meet a dwindling student demand.

Looking ahead, we expect that the required lower-division writing course will continue to serve fewer students (even as first-year classes grow). Consider the following estimates, all based on data from the UT Office of Institutional Reporting, Research, and Information Systems: between 2008 and 2013, an average of 3,700 students transferred RHE 306 credit per year. In 2012–13, roughly 44 percent of the incoming class had SAT scores high enough to allow them to test out of the required writing course. Based on these numbers, we can estimate that in an incoming class of 10,000 (not uncommon at UT), only 1,900 will need to take RHE 306 when they arrive at the university. And many of that remaining 1,900 may complete RHE 306 through a growing number of dual-credit high school classes supported by the state of Texas initiative to reduce the time to earn a college degree. All of these factors—test-out scores, transfer credit, and dual credit—conspire to reduce enrollment in RHE 306. In fall 2014, 514 students took RHE 306 in residence. In the fall of 2015, 453 students completed the class. This is a significant decline, but it is also typical. And the declining enrollment between 2014 and 2015 is even more remarkable when we consider the 2015–16 "superclass"—the largest first-year class in UT history—that frightened every administrator on the 40 acres. While other departments scrambled to accommodate a flood of students, the DRW anticipated lower enrollments in RHE 306. Because the demand for our required course is drying up, and the demand for elective lower-division writing classes has remained steady, the DRW has chosen to invest in the elective curriculum.

Though our lower-division budget has not been restored to its pre-2009 high, we are nowhere near the 2009 low either. Most important, the DRW's contribution to lower-division writing at UT Austin is increasing because we now offer a range of elective writing classes that cater to students' curricular needs and to their personal interests. In the end, we are still a service department, but we are no longer defined by the arduous (thankless and often joyless) chore of a required curriculum. We serve the university by offering classes that students both need and want.

THE RHETORIC AND WRITING MAJOR

The rhetoric and writing undergraduate major officially began in the fall of 2006. Its immediate success is demonstrated by the precipitous growth in the number of undergraduate majors. The program had enrolled 21 majors in January 2007, 140 majors in October 2008, 214 in September 2010, and 218 as of September 2016. Typically, there are between 175 and 200 rhetoric and writing majors. We are still considered a "small" major in the UT College of Liberal Arts. (In the spring of 2015, the largest major in COLA had 1,671 registered majors, the smallest had 6, and English, our nearest cognate discipline, had 947.) Nonetheless, college-level administrators are impressed by how quickly the major has grown.

The rhetoric and writing degree has been so successful because its lean structure permits double majoring, and because the courses appeal to undergraduates' intellectual interests. The twenty-seven hours of required coursework include a foundations course, at least one upper-division class in each of three general areas (history, theory, and digital media/technology), and at least one course focused on writing in specific situations (such as writing style, magazine writing, technical writing). An honors program with a capstone research project was added in 2013. The following course titles exhibit the appealing topics faculty choose to teach in their required courses in the major:

Media/Technology (RHE 330C)
   User-Centered Design
   Rhetoric and Serious Games
   Digital Storytelling

History (RHE 330D)
   Sophistry and the Invention of Rhetoric
   Rhetoric Invented, Revised, and Retold
   Arguing with Liberals

Theory and Analysis (RHE 330E)
   Comparative Rhetoric
   Pathos
   Demagoguery

In addition, we offer a suite of applied writing classes that complement students' professional and academic interests. Some of these courses are taught under the RHE 330C banner and others under course numbers, such as RHE 368C, RHE 360, RHE 325, and RHE 328. Rhetoric majors are required to take at least one upper-division applied writing course, but they may take others as electives. The following recent course titles exemplify this applied curriculum:

Grammar for Writers, Editors, and Teachers
Rhetoric and Writing for Teachers of English
Writing for Digital Media
Magazine Writing and Publishing
Writing for Nonprofits

A survey of alumni in summer 2016 shows great satisfaction with the major. The survey had a response rate of 31 percent from a current total of 323 alumni. The most frequent types of employment were legal, education, technology, and marketing/sales. Over three-quarters of respondents reported writing frequently or very frequently on the job, and over half gave oral presentations frequently or very frequently. Over 80 percent of respondents strongly agreed that majoring in rhetoric and writing increased their ability to read critically, write clearly, and write persuasively. Over two-thirds said it helped them figure out how to write in new situations. Some of the skills they considered most important on the job were writing to different audiences, acknowledging and responding to opposing positions, finding and using evidence to support claims, writing and revising collaboratively, editing their own and others' texts, and organizing ideas into coherent paragraphs and sections. Over half of alumni rated their training as excellent in all of these skills; over half also reported receiving excellent training in recognizing and deploying rhetorical strategies as well as critiquing print and online texts.

Alumni report considerable success in their careers: 22 percent of those who graduated before 2013 earn annual salaries of more than $100,000; another 18 percent earn more than $75,000. Even more pleasing are comments that reference rhetorical skills:

From day one on the job (and in life post-graduation), the emphasis that the rhetoric department puts on understanding your audience has been the greatest tool I've used. Understanding my audience—whether it be needy clients, overbearing attorneys, or bothersome coworkers—has helped me do my job competently. I've often received praise for handling different situations uniquely from my peers, but I feel I can give major credit to my Rhetoric degree and the critical thinking and analysis skills I learned in my Rhetoric classes. The more senior I become in my job, the more I find that I rely on tools I learned as an RHE major. Even now, as I find myself studying for the LSAT after all these years, the critical thinking skills and appreciation for varying perspectives have helped me tremendously in my studies.

This comment was echoed by several other alumni. We are happiest that our undergraduate major complements students' disciplinary interests and professional pursuits. Students who major and minor in rhetoric complete other degree programs and pursue a variety of careers, but they do so with the solid training in digital media, audience awareness, and persuasive composition that we provide.

THE DIGITAL WRITING AND RESEARCH LAB

In 2009, to better reflect the proliferation of small tech mobile devices that had begun to make up the technological landscape, the *Computer* Writing and Research Lab became the *Digital* Writing and Research Lab. Positioned at the intersection of rhetoric, writing, and technology, the DWRL is dedicated to the practice, teaching, and theory of emerging digital literacies. The DWRL hosts roughly eighty digitally oriented graduate and undergraduate rhetoric and literature courses per year in its five media classrooms, staffs an open media lab and regular skills workshops, and maintains a mentoring office where instructors teaching in the lab's classrooms or developing curricula for course proposals can go for assistance in developing, implementing, and assessing digital lesson plans and assignments.

As a result of budget cuts in 2015, the DWRL's staffing model downsized from about twenty-five part-time staffers, who worked seven hours per week on top of their teaching, to roughly nine staffers devoting a full twenty hours per week to the lab. The DWRL embraced this "downsizing" as an opportunity to sharpen its focus and commitment. What had been a series of discrete project sites were converted into a single content stream, broad research areas were explicitly articulated, and the mentoring task was more carefully defined.

Graduate students staffing the DWRL today offer instructional support and run in-class workshops on, for example, audio recording and editing, image editing, infographic production, and website development. Staffers engage in specific research projects that have resulted in the development and delivery of innovative lesson plans and curricular materials, which have inspired such undergraduate courses in the department as the Rhetoric of Facebook, the Rhetoric of Digital

Publishing, Rhetoric and Digital Life, Introduction to Visual Rhetoric, and the Rhetoric of Video Games. The College of Liberal Arts especially values the professional training the DWRL offers its staffers, who leave the lab with a wide array of digital skills and the confidence and competence to use them in pedagogical, scholarly, professional, and administrative endeavors.

In 2012, the DWRL launched the Digital Writing and Research Certificate program, which is designed to offer instructors a way to reflect on, organize, and showcase their expertise in the digital humanities. And in 2016, the DWRL developed the Digital Instruction Skills Certificate (DISC), which delivers seven online course modules devoted to digital instruction beyond the department, the college, and potentially the university. In fall 2020—in response to further budget cuts and to significant shifts in the job market—the DWRL will become the site of a studio-style, multi-semester practicum that will be required of all graduate students in the rhetoric concentration. This practicum will give our students, whatever their scholarly focus, the opportunity to learn and apply digital skills and research methods in their teaching and scholarship.

THE UNIVERSITY WRITING CENTER

Since 1993, the UWC has grown into one of the largest and busiest writing centers in the country, employing 125 consultants and conducting more than 11,000 writing consultations annually. Our consultants receive training in the non-directive, non-evaluative methods shaped by forty years of writing center research and practice. Since many of the graduate consultants go on to academic careers in the humanities, their experiences in the UWC will shape how universities across the United States teach writing.

In addition to the one-on-one consultations, UWC staff annually presents to more than 100 on-campus classes and cocurricular groups. We conduct workshops for community groups, especially K–12 groups from underrepresented schools. We manage and edit *Praxis: A Writing Center Journal*, a double-blind peer-reviewed journal on writing center pedagogy and practice. We hosted "The Future of Writing Centers," a 2012 symposium celebrating our twentieth anniversary. And we hosted the 2015 South Central Writing Centers Association Conference, with the theme "What Starts Here Writes the World."

These efforts have not gone unnoticed. In 2014, the College of Liberal Arts placed the UWC in the middle of an ambitious project: a

Learning Commons on the first floor of the Perry Castañeda Library. Co-funded by the Provost, the University of Texas Libraries, and the College of Liberal Arts, the Learning Commons colocates the UWC with library services, the Sanger Public Speaking Center, a state-of-the-art media lab, and active-learning spaces where Learning Commons partners offer presentations and workshops for UT classes and student groups.

The move to the Learning Commons more than doubled consultation space, produced a 12 percent increase in consultations annually, and enabled creative partnerships with our Learning Commons partners. It has also helped us attract funding (from the Vice Provost's Office and Graduate Studies, respectively) for two new initiatives: our Course Specialist Consultant Program, which embeds writing consultants in specific courses; and our Graduate Writing Services Program, which offers one-on-one consultations, writing groups, and writing retreats for University of Texas graduate students from all disciplines. Both programs have proved popular with students and faculty. Since much of the funding was temporary, our situation is good but fragile. We seek continued support to maintain current levels of service.

CONCLUSION

The DRW began as a division tending to a required, lower-division writing course. We have preserved that dedication to first-year writing, and we have become a valuable member of the university community—an irreplaceable part of undergraduate education—and a major source for graduate-student professionalization. We have made ourselves irreplaceable and indelible. Like every other department that is central to the university mission, we may be reduced, but we won't be eliminated; we may be cut, but we won't be cut out.

REFLECTION

Rather than becoming independent, the DRW has a continually shifting but viable degree of intra- and interdependence. With three units operating in different buildings across campus, we have had to work to keep centrifugal forces at bay. The DRW, UWC, and DWRL each has its own main office and staff, its own mission, and its own history of negotiations for funding from college and university administrators. The discipline of rhetoric and writing certainly looks different from each perspective. Our overall commitment to unity is partly a result of appointing unit directors who come from and return to the full-time departmental faculty and drawing staffers from the department's graduate assistant instructors and undergraduate majors. A high proportion of our faculty has administrative experience and can nimbly respond to external challenges and opportunities. At the college and university levels, what made the DRW a player rather than a pawn was achieving full-fledged department status with a popular undergraduate major. Departmental status has changed how we view transdisciplinarity, from a straw to clutch to for the sake of survival, to an extended branch that we can consider at arm's length. For example, our offer to expand the UWC's offerings to graduate students was taken up by the Graduate School and has evolved in productive ways. Our proposals to partner with departments in other colleges to develop multidisciplinary writing courses were received favorably at both the college and university levels. But these plans never garnered sufficient offers of financial support and remain undeveloped potentialities.

NOTE

Portions of this chapter were previously published: Longaker, Mark Garrett, Davida Charney, Diane Davis, and Alice Batt. 2016. "Growing despite Austerity: The Department of Rhetoric and Writing at the University of Texas at Austin." *College Composition and Communication* 68 (1), ed. Elizabeth Kalbfleisch, 185–91.

5

"AND SO TWO SHALL BECOME ONE"
Being (and Becoming) the School of Writing, Rhetoric and Technical Communication

Traci A. Zimmerman

On Valentine's Day 2008, the Writing and Rhetoric Program (W&R) was administratively merged with the Institute for Technical and Scientific Communication (ITSC), and the School of Writing, Rhetoric and Technical Communication (WRTC) at James Madison University was born. With this merger, two formerly distinct departments, each ten years old, each with faculty from a variety of academic and professional backgrounds, had to become one school. In so doing, we had to learn to see writing, rhetoric, and technical communication as one new creature, not two old creatures that now had to share the same living space. From this new perspective, we have begun to see how the questions of the past really come to bear on the possibilities of the present.

It is fitting that one of the predominant stories of St. Valentine is that of a failed conversion attempt: Valentine, persecuted as a Christian, is brought before Roman emperor Claudius II. The emperor, impressed by Valentine, attempts to convert him to paganism so that he might save his life. Valentine refuses and instead attempts to convert the emperor to Christianity (ostensibly) for the same goal: to save *his* life. We all know who wins this battle. (But who remembers Claudius II anymore?) In many ways, our Valentine's Day merger has mirrored this vexed conversion attempt: two different departments working to gain converts to "their side" so that their (professional) lives might be saved. But what has become evident over the last nine years is just how much we need each other, not only to survive, but to thrive.

Indeed, the "path" to the merger was longer than the e-mail that announced it, and it was paved with a series of important other transitions at both the college and university levels. First, it is important to note that the Writing Program (which would become Writing and Rhetoric Studies) was made possible by the fact that the newly formed

DOI: 10.7330/9781607328957.c005

College of Arts and Letters (1995–96) sought to substantially investigate the ways it should function to provide communication instruction writ large for its students. To do so, a faculty Communication Task Force was formed, and from its recommendations the dean created an autonomous Writing Program (to begin in the 1998–99 academic year), separate from the Department of English, with its own director, budget, tenure lines, and governance structure. This new program would be responsible for delivering the first-year writing courses (in the general education curriculum), but would also be charged with deepening the course offerings in rhetoric and composition to reflect the richness of the discipline and enhance the professional status of the writing curriculum and the composition faculty at JMU.

The Institute for Technical and Scientific Communication, by contrast, was developed, created, and approved by the State Council of Higher Education in Virginia (SCHEV) as a standalone program in 1997, though it is interesting that the author and champion of the proposal was the (then) department head of English, and it was the approval of this new institute (and the attendant questions of where to house it) that set into motion the dean's Communication Task Force investigation that would ultimately bring about the creation of the Writing Program.

Five years later, in 2002, the same dean who created the Writing Program (and applauded the approval of the ITSC) would evaluate the possibility of merging the two independent programs to form a larger and more stable unit within the college. After assembling a task force of faculty from both programs to investigate this potential path, and after numerous conversations with faculty from both programs, the dean decided to wait before proceeding with such a merger until each program had had the chance to stand for an Annual Program Review (APR). Having such an opportunity would allow each of the programs to conduct an internal self-study, as well as go through an external review process—a crucial balance of agency and assessment—that would give a clearer picture of where the strengths, weaknesses, and opportunities for future growth lay.

Approximately two years later, it was announced that the Schools of Art and Art History, Music, and Theatre and Dance would be leaving the College of Arts and Letters to become their own College of Visual and Performing Arts (CVPA), which would eventually be launched in the 2006–7 academic year. With that announcement, the remaining ten units in the College of Arts and Letters and its new dean were given a unique opportunity to think about the future of the college and their role in it. Discussions began and task forces formed to explore possible futures. From them emerged the frameworks for three distinct divisions of the college: the School of Public and International Affairs (international affairs, political science, justice studies, and public policy and administration); the School of Liberal Arts (English, history, foreign languages, sociology/anthropology, and philosophy/religion); and the Schools of Communication, Information, and Media (communication studies, media arts and design, writing and rhetoric studies, and the Institute for Technical and Scientific Communication). And, once again, the question of a possible merger between the ITSC and the now Writing and Rhetoric Studies Program emerged, but with a different context and urgency: of the ten units in the College of Arts and Letters, W&R was the only unit without a major, a decided disadvantage when coming to the bargaining table. Still, it would take another four years before the announcement came—at 10:28 a.m. on Valentine's Day, 2008—that Writing and Rhetoric Studies and the Institute for Technical and Scientific Communication would be merged to form a new unit in the college.

As a school formed from the top down (rather than from the ground up), one of the initial challenges we faced was how to cultivate a shared identity between two units that were very proud (and protective) of their independent status before the merger. How do we make decisions about what courses to keep, delete, or modify? How do we envision a curricular identity that is both protective of what we value and prescient about future growth? How do we create an environment where faculty can meaningfully contribute to something they may not have envisioned or desired?

Before the merger, the ITSC offered an undergraduate major and minor as well as a master's degree; W&R offered only a minor. After the merger, W&R faculty inherited a major and a master's program (literally) overnight, while the small ITSC faculty of five gained twenty-two new full-time colleagues. As one might expect, our new unit was at first fraught with programmatic and practical hurdles, not the least of which was deciding what to call ourselves. That problem was solved democratically, and not altogether unpleasantly, at a dinner hosted by the college, where these two formerly distinct groups of faculty gathered for the first time as colleagues. Together, we worked through a number of possibilities (as well as through our anxieties), struggling with whether (and how much) we should import from our past(s), wondering if we should just start from a completely different point on the map. Ultimately, after sifting through the ideas that grew out of our dinner meeting and voting by secret ballot, what emerged was that "writing," "rhetoric," and "technical communication" were too vital to lose and that they were elements around which we all could rally. But we also knew, even if we didn't articulate it at the time, that we were going to have to understand and operationalize these terms in an entirely different context; that is, we could not just use them as comfortable "defaults" to continue "business as usual."

The necessity for this "new" understanding became evident as we faced our next obstacle: how to work with a curriculum necessarily (but hastily) pieced together rather than integrated toward a common goal. Admittedly and understandably, the first two years of the curriculum were distinguished by a number of irregularities: requirement inconsistencies, management incongruity, illogical course distribution, awkward course sequencing, along with some course duplications, redundancies, and the like. We knew it was essential that WRTC's undergraduate curriculum be restructured to address shared academic objectives so we could avoid operating as the School of Writing, Rhetoric *or* Technical Communication and instead become the School of Writing, Rhetoric *and* Technical Communication. Where we had an advantage was that we were an entirely new unit, not only to JMU but also to the Commonwealth of Virginia; as such, we enjoyed a rare opportunity to repackage the circumstances that created us into avenues for curriculum innovation and programmatic leadership. It is precisely because of our status as an independent unit that we had the space and support to innovate and invent our new curriculum. Though we were formed from the top down, our independent status allowed us to (re)build the program from the ground up. The benefits of our independent and interdisciplinary status in these endeavors cannot be overstated. The most challenging restriction we encountered was time.

To help us move quickly but responsibly, the dean immediately assembled a Transition Committee to help us work through the logistics of curriculum delivery, advising, and management. We had to be able to honor the course plans of current students, as well as to design a cohesive (but temporary) plan for incoming majors. Beyond the practical concerns of keeping the school moving forward were the philosophical concerns of how we could learn to work together, toward a goal we may never have envisioned, in a department none of us were hired into. Despite these challenges, we still managed to deliver a competitive major because of the commitment of a dedicated faculty. But we had no illusions about the future: we knew that the WRTC needed to put its curricular house in order. We also understood that the only way forward was to move together, as a unit, through collaboration and consensus.

So, as a whole unit, early in the spring semester of 2011, we approached the enormous task of creating the new WRTC curriculum in small teams, intensively and inclusively. We created larger groups around the two concentrations—writing and rhetoric, and technical and scientific communication—aligning faculty expertise within these teaching areas and assigning each faculty member as a "primary" to one or two courses. It was important for us to view this work through the lens of creation more than through that of revision; that is, we didn't just want to smash two courses together and call it a "new" thing. Admittedly, our default start position was exactly that: kind of a one-part "spring cleaning" of old or (now) defunct courses, and a one-part "mix-and-mash," where we pulled out elements of old familiar courses and repackaged them as "new and improved." But as each faculty member connected with their teams about their courses, and those teams re-visioned and refashioned the raw material—passing them to the concentration groups and then, ultimately, to the full faculty for review and feedback—the "new" began to emerge. The process was necessarily imperfect, since we were designing courses for an "audience invoked," in anticipation for a future unknown but hoped for. But what made it a success is that we went through it together; literally every person in the unit worked on singular courses within specific units but was then encouraged to give feedback on every course. At the end of this process, in late fall 2011, we voted—unanimously—to approve the curriculum we had created.

Michel Foucault (1972, 223) reminds us, "For a discipline to exist, there must be the possibility of formulating—and of doing so ad infinitum—fresh propositions." In some ways, the merger forced this kind of formulation. What we are working on now is not how to redefine ourselves based on our past identities but how to define and develop "the new." I would argue that we are doing the work of "revolutionary change" (*pace* Thomas Kuhn)—work that "is defined in part by its difference from normal change, and normal change is . . . the sort that results in growth, accretion, cumulative addition to what was known before . . . Revolutionary changes are different as they involve discoveries that cannot be accommodated within the concepts in use before they were made . . . *One cannot get from the old to the new simply by an addition to what was already known*" (Kuhn 2000, 14–15; emphasis added).

Revolutionary change is neither swift nor easily comprehended, and so we continually seek to create identity and mission, strategy and coherence, relevance and depth. Ironically, our being formed in the midst of the 2008 financial crisis was ideal timing for the work that lay ahead, as we had to immediately and substantially address the criticisms of higher education that then (and now) claimed that colleges are unjustifiably expensive, largely unaccountable, and widely inaccessible, and that they have failed in their key mission to educate and prepare students for their futures. Certainly, these "value-added" arguments are not new (as anyone who works in a large state institution can attest), but they are indeed viable lenses through which legislators, administrators, and potential students view the work of "the university." Implicit in our curriculum redesign was the question of how best to address these critiques in a way that would still allow us to protect and advance what we value about higher education: fostering a spirit of intellectual agility, providing a lens of critical inquiry, and encouraging the practice of thoughtful humanity. And so we worked to build a plan of study that addresses the ever-changing landscape of mobile, mediated, and networked communication by anchoring those studies in what I like to call "the things that stay": the contingencies and contexts of language, the enduring questions of identity, ethics, and representation, and the real challenges of communicating and collaborating with others.

An advantage we had in our curricular pursuits is that the WRTC, though new, was already well-situated in the larger university community. The old Writing and Rhetoric Program had been offering (for over a decade) approximately 150 sections of WRTC 103: Critical Reading and Writing, a required course in the General Education Program, to more than 3,000 students a year. The WRTC 103 course and our connection to the General Education Program remains a priority within the WRTC, though the added demands of delivering a major, a minor, and a graduate program constantly challenge us to think creatively and strategically about how to support all our academic programs. Our major courses are also affiliated with several multidisciplinary minors at JMU as well as with two study abroad programs, and our community-based learning courses (a requirement for all our majors) connect our students to the surrounding community in valuable and visible ways. As an interdisciplinary unit, we tend to seek out collaborative interactions with units across campus; these interactions energize our work and promote engagement with, and investment in, the academic enterprise writ large. Indeed, it is our interdisciplinarity as much as our independent status that keeps us agile, and though our initial concerns about merging were centered largely on what would be *lost* in that exchange, we can see now all that has been gained.

As the WRTC concludes its first decade, we can claim some successes: we collaboratively redeveloped and re-envisioned the entire undergraduate and graduate curriculum; we formed an Alumni Council, the majority of whom were not part of WRTC but were graduates of its for-mer units (ITSC/W&R), who have not only embraced but championed the new school; and we have hired eight new faculty members who enrich and catalyze our work. We have also enjoyed a bit of fortuitous *kairos* in that our new curriculum debuted in the same year as our new university president, who in 2014 would unveil his new vision for James Madison University: "To be the national model of the engaged univer-sity: engaged with ideas and the world." Our new curriculum—with its required internship, required community-based learning elective, numerous practicum opportunities, and courses designed to balance theory and praxis—aligned immediately with the University Vision, providing a way to institutionally validate and support the work we do. Ironically, it was our being formed in the midst of the Great Recession that forced us to think carefully about our resources, about what we value and why, and about how we could design a sustainable, mean-ingful program that would both educate and inspire; and it was these less than ideal circumstances that ended up positioning us well within the institution.

David Beard (2010, 145) wrote in *What We Are Becoming* that "the historical moments in which freestanding rhetoric programs can exist are vanishing." And at first glance, Beard would appear to be right in his estimation when it comes to the WRTC; after all, we were created by dismantling two independent programs. But the clearing away of these old structures has allowed us to apprehend the new and to (as our logo states) "Envision, Create, Communicate." The new space also allows us to see our way forward and to anticipate the world into which our students will enter college and the world that will await them when they leave.

Our story of "being and becoming" the School of Writing, Rhetoric and Technical Communication is one that likely shares some of the same challenges as those of other independent writing programs, though our path be marked with peaks and valleys: our independence was won, then lost, then regained. As we move into the next decade, we see more opportunities than we do obstacles because we have the resources, infra-structure, and freedom that allow us to do so. It certainly helps that we have had tremendous support at both the college and university levels and that our curriculum aligns with the institutional mission and vision. But at the core of our growth and success has been the willingness of the WRTC faculty to consistently evolve, to always connect, to challenge their "defaults" with the occasional "hard reset," and to think about how best to practice and teach that which is simultaneously ever-changing and steeped in history. What has become abundantly clear is that we needed each other to remain independent.

REFLECTION

Throughout this book, "independent" is used repeatedly to describe the programs and departments represented. But this description is more nuanced and complex than it might first appear; that is, "independent" should not be read as meaning merely the opposite of "dependent" in these cases. No independent writing program or independent writing department can operate on an island, remaining aloof to the many structures of support on which it depends. The WRTC is one of ten units in the College of Arts and Letters, and we operate in concert with (not in service to) those other units. We have our own governance structures, our own hiring lines, and control over our curriculum. Still, we understand this ownership (and our "independence") as a collective rather than an individualistic enterprise. Just as the term *independent* cannot be understood outside the context of "dependence"—(what, after all, are you independent of, independent from?)—we have to understand "independent writing programs" in an appropriate context: perhaps as "interdependent writing programs" that exist among, contribute to, and rely on a network (rather than a "niche") to thrive. Independence is more than becoming unencumbered by other masters. It is the opportunity to live and develop according to the best possible or natural potentials. In our case, there is more than merely the idea that we can teach writing, rhetoric, and technical communication. Instead, they are the means by which we can reach forward and create individual and collective futures. We set agendas and advocate for them. We lead by articulating possibilities. Our independence allows us to pursue them.

REFERENCES

Beard, David. 2010. "Dancing with Our Siblings: The Unlikely Case for a Rhetoric Major." In *What We Are Becoming: Developments in Undergraduate Writing Majors,* ed. Greg A. Gibson and Thomas A. Moriarty, 130–52. Logan: Utah State University Press.

Foucault, Michel. 1972. *The Archaeology of Knowledge and the Discourse on Language.* Trans. A. M. Sheridan Smith. New York: Pantheon Books.

Kuhn, Thomas. 2000. *The Road since Structure: Philosophical Essays, 1970–1993, with an Autobiographical Interview.* Ed. James Conant and John Haugeland. Chicago: University of Chicago Press.

6

THE GREAT RECESSION
Helping and Hurting Writing Faculty in an Independent Writing Program

Richard N. Matzen Jr.

The Great Recession—which in 2008 gripped the country and pushed "California deep into a fiscal crisis" (Kelderman 2012)—created increased student enrollment and sustained faculty development opportunities in the Writing Department at Woodbury University, a small, private, nonprofit, non-denominational university in Burbank, California. Then, in the fall of 2013, the university's enrollment dropped significantly. For the first time in its existence, Woodbury University and its Writing Department felt the Great Recession's economic pressure, five years after the Great Recession started.

This chapter, subsequently, describes how Woodbury University's independent Writing Department evolved its writing programs and faculty development opportunities—for both part- and full-time faculty members—between 2005 and 2013, perhaps a golden era for Woodbury writing faculty in retrospect. Then, after explaining how the department lost approximately half its budget, the chapter examines why, even after launching a new professional writing degree, the Writing Department lives with an uncertain future.

Overall, the story of Woodbury University's Writing Department may mean that wiser writing program administrators continually explore alternative writing program structures in order to survive, if not thrive. This exploration, however, includes uncertainty. For example, the Writing Department's history suggests that during positive economic times, part-time writing faculty were foundational in the department's writing programs; however, eventually, as a consequence of the Great Recession, the part-time faculty's presence in the writing programs diminished, creating uncertainty for them and for the department as a whole. At the same time, the department's full-time faculty members' status, if not their professional identities, shifted because of

DOI: 10.7330/9781607328957.c006

launching the new professional writing degree. But in spite of answering Maxine Hairston's 1985 Conference on College Composition and Communication (CCCC) call for more independent writing programs and Kathleen Yancey's 2004 CCCC call for more undergraduate degrees in writing, Woodbury's Writing Department's full-time faculty found their jobs less secure in 2017, as the national trend for small liberal arts universities losing students seemed to continue (Quintana and Hatch 2017).

WOODBURY UNIVERSITY, RECESSION ECONOMICS, AND STUDENT ENROLLMENT

To better understand how the Great Recession affected Woodbury's Writing Department, fuller descriptions of the university and the department need to be joined to a deeper understanding of how California students transfer from community colleges to both private and public universities.

In general, Woodbury University is tuition-dependent, that is, dependent on enrollment for finances. Its student body, as defined by the fall 2014 semester, is typical of its past and present cultural diversity, in that no single cultural group dominates: 5 percent African American, 9 percent Asian American, 25 percent Hispanic American students, and 39 percent European American (approximately half are Armenian American), plus 21 percent international students (Woodbury University Institutional Research 2017). In addition, approximately 70 percent of all students are first-generation college students (Boglioli 2012), and the university is a federally designated Hispanic-serving institution.

Consequently, at Woodbury University, the economics of *transfer credit* may be understood as providing access to higher education for minority and first-generation college students. From the transfer student's perspective, the economic plan here is to complete as many transferable general education (or liberal arts) credits as possible at a more affordable community college and then transfer those credits to a university, possibly the equivalent of an associate of arts (AA) degree (i.e., sixty credit hours). Approximately two-thirds of Woodbury students are transfer students who typically begin their university education as second-semester sophomores or first-semester juniors. This transfer phenomenon means that Woodbury University was at first insulated from the Great Recession and even benefited from it.

In 2009, as *Chronicle* reporter Josh Keller (2009b, 2009c, 2009d) explained, because of a lack of state funding—caused by the Great

Table 6.1. Woodbury University's total student enrollment

Semester	Student Enrollment
Fall 2008	1,546
Fall 2009	1,614
Fall 2010	1,628
Fall 2011	1,557
Fall 2012	1,771 (+214)
Fall 2013	1,607 (−164)
Fall 2014	1,590 (−17)
Fall 2015	1,457 (−133)
Fall 2016	1,283 (−174)
Fall 2017	1,160 (−123)

Source: Woodbury University Institutional Research 2017.

Table 6.2. Writing Department's combined enrollment in WRIT 100, 111, 112, and 212

Semester	Total Student Enrollment in WRIT Courses
Fall 2008	253
Fall 2009	292 (+39)
Fall 2010	341 (+49)
Fall 2011	389 (+48)
Fall 2012	482 (+93)
Fall 2013	317 (−165)
Fall 2014	349 (−32)
Fall 2015	300 (−49)
Fall 2016	304 (+4)
Fall 2017	241 (−63)

Source: Woodbury University Writing Department 2017.

Recession—the University of California, California State University, and California community college systems drastically reduced their student enrollments. By October 2009, because of budget cuts and not enough classes being offered, California students had these options: stay at a community college, attend a private university, or drop out (Keller 2009a). So with admission to, and degree completion at, the University of California and California State University frustrated—as well as unavailable seats at the community colleges—Keller predicted that California students would increasingly attend private universities. This proved to be the case at Woodbury University.

Although enrollments in California's higher education system continued to shrink through 2011 (Keller 2011), Woodbury's enrollment remained relatively steady between 2008 and 2011 (table 6.1). Then, in the fall of 2012, the university experienced an unexpected positive effect of the Great Recession. A record 1,771 students enrolled: 1,424 undergraduate, 283 graduate, and 64 non-degree-seeking students (Woodbury University Institutional Research 2017).

However, in November 2012, after California voters approved Proposition 30, the state legislature restored some funds to community colleges. By 2013, community colleges had significantly increased their available seats in transferable general education courses (Huckabee 2013); subsequently, Woodbury's fall 2013 enrollment diminished by 164 students (Woodbury University Institutional Research 2017), beginning the trend of declining enrollments. Or, in other words, the previous transfer plan of attending community college and transferring credits to a university had re-started by the fall of 2013.

The Great Recession, moreover, affected enrollments in Woodbury University's writing courses: basic writing (WRIT 100), essay writing (WRIT 111), and research writing (WRIT 112 or WRIT 212). At the beginning of the Great Recession, the WRIT enrollment increased progressively from 2008 to 2012 (table 6.2). In the fall of 2012, as university enrollment bubbled, the WRIT enrollment bubbled too, to 482 students. Thereafter, in the fall of 2013, WRIT enrollment fell, beginning what would be a near-steady decline to the present (table 6.2).

After the bubble burst, Woodbury students nevertheless benefited from the Great Recession because of a progressive increase in scholarships and financial aid for students. This mirrored national trends. The *Chronicle of Higher Education* reported that the average *net* price for tuition and fees at four-year nonprofit colleges "dipped during and following the Great Recession of 2007–9 because the federal government poured additional money into financial aid" ("Published and Net Tuition Fees" 2014). In 2013–14, the average *published* tuition and fees at four-year private nonprofit colleges were $30,090; however, that same year, students' *net* tuition and fees totaled $12,460 ("Published and Net Tuition Fees" 2014).

BEFORE THE GREAT RECESSION: WOODBURY UNIVERSITY'S INDEPENDENT WRITING PROGRAM

In the 1985 CCCC chair's address, Maxine Hairston (1985, 273) discusses why rhetoric and composition colleagues may want to create programs independent of their literature colleagues: "Within individual institutions . . . we often find ourselves confronting the literature faculty who dominate so many departments, and we feel that we are fighting losing battles: battles to get hard money to staff the writing center, battles to establish programs for training writing teachers, or battles against staffing composition courses with under paid, low-status part-timers." One reason to admire Hairston's address is that it's still relevant today in spite of passing decades.

Its relevance to Woodbury University, however, is ironic. Woodbury University never possessed an English department, in spite of offering literature courses. But historically and perhaps more aligned with Hairston's thinking, MA, MFA, or PhD literature degree holders have taught the majority of the writing (WRIT) courses at Woodbury.

This has been the case at least since 2005, when I began working at Woodbury.

At that time, I was hired because of my background in rhetoric and composition (rhet/comp) to create and direct a writing center, to revitalize and direct the first-year composition courses (WRIT 111 and WRIT 112/212), and to initiate a writing across the curriculum (WAC)/writing in the disciplines (WID) program—all without any graduate students or teaching assistants. So Woodbury's independent writing program began in 2005 with my hiring and with the WRIT courses being removed from the Humanities Department. The Humanities Department itself ceased to exist then, too. Its diverse courses were disbursed into other programs and departments. From 2005 to 2013, I was the only full-time rhet/comp trained professor in the writing program. During that time, the Writing Department employed between seven and fifteen part-time professors. Between 46 percent and 67 percent of the faculty held degrees (and training) above the MA level: MFA, PhD, or DM degrees. Expertise in teaching English to speakers of other languages (TESOL), creative writing, business, and interdisciplinary studies existed among our faculty group, meaning that the literature-trained professors did not exclusively define us.

Adjunct Pay and Faculty Opportunities

To attract part-time English faculty, the Writing Department's 2012 summer ad in the *Chronicle of Education* gave potential applicants a snapshot of adjunct work conditions ("Chronicle Ad—Writing Adjunct Professors" 2012). For example, although the maximum capacity of a single WRIT class (WRIT 111, 112, 212) was twenty students, the ad accurately stated that the average WRIT class size was fifteen students. Also, as read in the ad, adjunct pay ranged from $2,850 to $3,080 for a three-credit course, and adjuncts were expected to participate in two to three paid workshops per semester regarding curriculum, technology, and assessment, which cumulatively increased their pay by $400 to $800 per semester. The ad mentioned, moreover, that select adjuncts were offered $2,600 for working approximately forty hours per semester as writing consultants in the WAC/WID program. These consultants typically worked as coteachers of courses. Additional opportunities existed for adjuncts to work as raters in the English Placement Program and to participate in the department's assessing of papers written by undergraduate and graduate students in the School of Business. For some years, too, adjuncts could earn as much as $1,000 if all stages of the department's hybrid/online certification program were completed. In other words, the Writing Department provided significant faculty development and professional experience opportunities to adjuncts, which better qualified them to teach at Woodbury or elsewhere.

In addition, between 2005 and 2013, the Writing Department selected three adjuncts to be Participating Adjuncts, which meant that all three worked contemporaneously, received a course release each fall and spring semester, and were guaranteed a certain number of WRIT courses to teach. Their collective responsibilities meant that they helped coordinate and administrate the English Placement Program, the Writing Awards Program, the Writing Center, and the Writing Consultant Program (WCP). Within the WCP, a WAC/WID program, adjuncts were also hired to either work one-on-one with select students on their discipline-specific writing (i.e., to conduct tutorials) or to teach extended workshops in select courses, usually in the School of Business. For two academic years (2012–13 and 2013–14), the WCP budget was more than twice the size of the Writing Center budget. In 2013–14, twenty-two business courses and five writing professors were involved in the WCP. The Writing Department's opportunities for adjuncts—which included writing program administrator work—eventually qualified one part-time faculty member to become a dean at a nearby community college.

The teaching and administrative labor adjuncts provided created opportunities for the department's two full-time professors as well. Between 2005 and 2010, Will McConnell, a PhD in interdisciplinary studies, and I directed the Writing Center; conducted annual assessment plans; supervised participating adjuncts; wrote curricular proposals; taught and co-taught select non-WRIT courses; created and maintained collaborations with area community colleges; completed discipline and university program reviews; and piloted new WRIT courses, tutorial services, Writing Center curriculum, bridge programs, and an e-portfolio system. We also performed more traditional duties: constructing and maintaining budgets and class schedules, hiring and evaluating adjuncts (and writing center tutors), observing and evaluating faculty members, and making data-driven administrative decisions. In these ways, we supervised all the department's writing programs: the English Placement Program, Writing Awards, Writing Center, the Writing Consultant Program, the WRIT 112 Transfer Portfolio Program, and the Hybrid-Online Certification Program. When Dr. McConnell left the Writing Program to chair the Interdisciplinary Studies Department in 2010, newly hired Dr. Reuben Ellis and I completed these responsibilities until 2013.

Writing Successes

In 2010, the Western Association of Schools and Colleges (WASC) accreditation team made its campus visit. In their report, while citing the university's exemplary programs and departments, they praised the writing programs' assessment (WASC 2010, 22, 27–28), classified the WRIT portfolio system as "highly developed" (31), and commended the writing programs for integrating adjuncts into assessment processes (36–37). The writing programs' next successes were found in two program reviews. First, in 2010–11, working with the Council of Writing Program Administrators' (CWPA) consultants-evaluators, the Writing Department conducted a self-study and organized the consultants-evaluators' two-day campus visit. The consultants-evaluators' 2011 report rightly pointed out some areas of improvement: improve multimodal composition instruction and the WRIT learning outcomes, for example. Thereafter, this program review became the basis for a more extensive university-level program review conducted in 2012–13. The Writing Department submitted that larger program review to the university's Educational Planning Committee. While endorsing the CWPA consultants-evaluators' recommendations, the Educational Planning Committee (2013) commended the Writing Department for its assessment, integration of adjuncts into department processes, expansion of tutorial services through the WCP, and partnerships with other university departments and programs. The Educational Planning Committee (2013, 3) concluded, "Overall, your program has accomplished a great deal of work with very limited resources." Successful program reviews, among other activities, enabled the Writing Program to become the Writing Department in 2011.

In 2012, the Writing Department successfully created a new English as a second language (ESL) program along with a full-time administrative assistant position and a new full-time visiting professor position for the ESL program. That year, too, the department's WCP earned praise for contributing in the areas of writing assessment and writing-intensive course development in the undergraduate and graduate business curricula. In fact, our contributions here helped the Business School earn AASCB (Association to Advance Collegiate Schools of Business) accreditation in 2014, the highest accreditation possible for a business school ("AACSB Accredited" 2018).

Between 2005 and 2014, the Writing Department's success was also mirrored by five adjuncts—all with literature degrees—who became full-time English professors at Los Angeles–area universities and community colleges. The adjuncts' successes, in other words, resulted in part from the department providing them with substantive faculty development and professional experience opportunities.

THE GREAT RECESSION: DOWN AND UP SIDES FOR WOODBURY UNIVERSITY AND ITS INDEPENDENT WRITING PROGRAM/DEPARTMENT

After the summer of 2013, I stepped down as Writing Department chair to develop my research and scholarship and to return to creative writing, a change I had been planning for some years. When the new chair, Reuben Ellis, began that fall, the university was facilitating cost reductions because of low enrollment (table 6.1). Between 2013 and 2015, the WCP and the ESL program were eliminated. Also, the assistant chair, visiting professor/ESL director, and Participating Adjuncts positions were eliminated. Then, too, the remaining possible stipends for adjuncts—for participating in a few faculty meetings and an assessment session—were reduced to one-third of their former value. At one point, the Writing Center was threatened with closure but was preserved. By 2017, not surprisingly, all administrative aspects of WRIT courses—for example, placement, registration, transfer portfolios, adjunct contracts—were to be completed by the one administrator left in the Writing Department, the chair (or co-chairs).

On the upside, through the leadership of Professor Ellis, the Writing Department successfully proposed a professional writing degree in 2014. The upper administration supported the new degree in part as a way to counteract the emerging negative effects of the Great Recession. Subsequently, the Writing Department was allowed to hire a new full-time rhet/comp faculty member, Matthew Bridgewater, PhD, who began in the fall of 2014. The launch of the new professional writing degree in the fall of 2016, however, did not create a boom in enrollment for the Writing Department or for the university: five professional writing majors and two minors defined the first cohort in the Professional Writing Program.

Meanwhile, under new presidential leadership that began in the fall of 2015, the university aggressively eliminated numerous staff, administrative, and faculty positions. One rationale for the personnel cuts was that fewer positions were needed, given that the student enrollment had shrunk. Positions ranging from vice president positions down to staff positions were eliminated, with Student Affairs (i.e., student support services) losing the most positions. Subsequently, what had been routine processes—in the Admissions, Business, Registrar's, and Student Affairs Offices—became "new" processes with complications that often required repeated efforts to work. Also, between 2012 and 2017, the university decreased full-time faculty positions from approximately ninety to sixty-five. This was done mostly through incentivized early retirement plans, not renewing visiting professor positions, and not filling faculty positions that were vacated by professors who had left to work elsewhere.

In 2017, the creation of the Enrollment Management Committee—composed of staff, faculty, and administrators—defined another of the university's major efforts to curtail operating with a financial deficit. With the guidance of outside consultants, this new committee was to make data-driven decisions regarding recruitment, curriculum, and services. Essentially, many of the substantive new expenditures in these areas needed to be justified as having a positive predictive impact on student enrollment and university finances. Beginning in the summer of 2017, I served a one-year term on the Enrollment Management Committee, and in its first year, the committee considered dozens of action plans before approving approximately ten for implementation.

Unfortunately, after absorbing the delayed effects of the Great Recession, Woodbury University was also caught in the grip of a national trend, somewhat heralded in this 2017 *Chronicle of Higher Education* headline: "177 Private Colleges Fail Education Dept.'s Financial-Responsibility Test." Therein, Chris Quintana and Joshua Hatch (2017) wrote that "177 private colleges that grant degrees failed a U.S. Education Department test for financial responsibility in the 2014–15 academic year." Of the 177, 122 were nonprofit institutions.

Nevertheless, because of the previously cited financial efforts, Woodbury University fortunately returned to a balanced budget during the 2017–18 fiscal year. Also, the fall of 2018 enrollment demonstrated the first increase in enrollment since the fall of 2012 and, it is hoped, ended the enrollment decline (table 6.1). Another positive is that Woodbury University ranked fourteenth in terms of economic value out of 110 small colleges in California and in the top 4 percent nationally for colleges and universities ("Rankings" 2017).

THREE ARGUMENTS FOR PROFESSIONAL WRITING

Nevertheless, at Woodbury University, a crisis atmosphere persists in which the value of liberal arts degrees—as compared to architecture, film, animation, and graphic design degrees—and under-enrolled professional degree programs is questioned. Hence, during 2017 and 2018, the question emerged as to the value of the professional writing curriculum given that professional writing only had six majors at the end of spring 2018. Subsequently, early in the summer, the Writing Department co-chairs created three arguments to, it was hoped, transform a seemingly rhetorical question into a substantive one.

First, in part through an alliance with the Department of Communication, the number of under-enrolled professional writing courses decreased in the spring of 2018. In other words, that spring, professional writing students enrolled in select courses in other disciplines, for example, Screenwriting One (Filmmaking Department) and Digital Journalism (Department of Communication), knowing that these courses would fulfill professional writing requirements in either the major or minor. Also, during the spring 2018 semester, professional writing students were advised to consider enrolling in Introduction to Social Media, a communication course, when registering for fall 2018 classes. In addition, regarding the spring 2019 class schedules, the Writing Department created a plan with the Department of Communication in which professional writing students would not only be advised to register for select communication courses (for professional writing credit), but also communication students would be advised to enroll in select professional writing courses (for communication credit). These current and future plans, which include collaboratively redesigning a COMM and a WRIT course, in other words, would not only limit the under-enrolled professional writing classes but would also add students to select communication and professional writing classes.

In some ways, the second argument extends the first. That is, because fewer under-enrolled sections of professional writing courses occur, an acceptable average enrollment for *all* WRIT classes, including first-year composition classes, is better maintained. Setting aside a few one-student WRIT courses—internship credits and directed studies credits—the average WRIT class size in the fall of 2017 and spring 2018 was sixteen students, an acceptable average for Woodbury. This positive average and perpetuating it, however, depends on the writing program administrator, that is, the co-chairs or chair, filling WRIT 111 and 112 sections to capacity, which they did and will continue to do.

The third argument for retaining the professional writing degree is that although the number of total majors increased by one, comparing the fall 2016 number to the spring 2018 number, the number of professional writing minors tells a different story. Their numbers increased from two in the fall of 2016 to approximately twelve for the fall of 2018. Moreover, the numbers of professional writing minors are expected to continue to increase because Writing Department faculty will continue to recruit new minors from their WRIT 112 classes and because of the successful launch of a national online literary journal, *Moria*, in the fall of 2017, a real draw for new minors.

DEALING WITH ECONOMIC FALLOUT

Within the Writing Department, the three full-time faculty members and the Writing Center director agree that during the 2018–19 academic year, the professional writing curriculum needs to be modified. They also agree that the presence of creative writing courses in the curriculum should increase because current professional writing majors and minors, as well as possible recruits, have requested more creative writing courses. Furthermore, regarding spring 2019, communication majors will be advised to enroll in the WRIT introductory creative writing course to satisfy requirements in their communication degree. The spring 2019 Professional Writing courses are the introductory creative writing course, the *Moria* course, a fiction writing course, and a legal and policy writing course.

Nevertheless, at the time of this writing, at least one full-time professional writing faculty member doubts the worthiness of collaborating more with the Department of Communication and fears that this collaboration compromises the meaning and integrity of the professional writing curriculum. At the same time, the Writing Department does not know if the previous three arguments for the professional writing curriculum will prevent upper administrators from suspending it. In other words, Woodbury University's professional writing program has to admit that it depends not only on its own faculty members but also on its own institution for a future. Fortunately, at this time, no one seriously questions the validity of first-year writing courses.

REFLECTION

Like other writing program administrators, I have sought, found, and built alliances with faculty members in other disciplines and with staff members who help deliver student support services. For me, at least two sources support these alliances. The first source is my knowledge, training, and experience with WAC/WID, which guide first-year writing courses as well. Nevertheless, my working with faculty in other disciplines seems challenged by how well we agree on shared intellectual frameworks and terminology for our collaboration. My second support for alliances derives from sharing a language with bridge program, ESL program, and writing center collaborators based on held-in-common terminology or reviews of literature. However, stepping outside of such specific discourse communities to explain and share a program's value and goals with non-English faculty and upper administrators, for example, creates new situations in which shared intellectual frameworks and agreed-upon terms can be problematic.

At present, ironically in part because of this book, I am cultivating a greater willingness to let my own disciplinary knowledge rest while increasing my effort to put myself in my collaborators' shoes by more readily accepting their disciplinary knowledge and using what I hope are more neutral but informative terms to describe collaborations: interdisciplinarity, multidisciplinarity, and transdisciplinarity (Repko, Szostak, and Phillips Buchberger 2013). Currently, for example, multidisciplinary (Repko, Szostak, and Phillips Buchberger 2013, 35) describes the relationship between the communication and professional writing curricula: professional writing students can draw on two disciplines at times to understand one communicative phenomenon. However, upcoming collaborations—such as collaboratively revising a select course with communication faculty—may rise to the level of *interdisciplinarity*, that is, truly integrating two disciplines to create a new understanding of a problem (Repko, Szostak, and Phillips Buchberger 2013, 35); or to the level of *transdisciplinarity*, that is, applying various disciplinary perspectives for creating a real greater public good (36). Said another way, the old WAC/WID language may not well describe the emerging curricular relationships between the Writing and Communication Departments. Why not consider the possibility that "new" academic terms may make me a more effective collaborator with colleagues within and outside of writing studies?

REFERENCES

"AACSB Accredited." 2018. http:///www.woodbury.edu/program/school-of-business/.

Boglioli, Bonnie. 2012. "Woodbury University's Dori Littell-Herrick Discusses Woodbury's Program, Her Own Career and Observations of the Industry." *Dave School*, May 12. http://www.daveschool.com.

"Chronicle Ad—Writing Adjunct Professors." 2012. *Chronicle of Higher Education* (May–June).

CWPA Consultants-Evaluators. 2011. "External Review of the Writing Department at Woodbury University." Unpublished report, September.

Educational Planning Committee. 2013. "Response to Writing Program Review." Unpublished memo, February 6.

Hairston, Maxine. 1985. "Breaking Our Bonds and Reaffirming Our Connections." *College Composition and Communication* 36 (3): 272–82.

Huckabee, Charles. 2013. "Calif. Community Colleges Note a Positive Trend: More Summer Courses." *Chronicle of Higher Education* (May 16). http://www.chronicle.com/blogs/ticker/calif-community-colleges-note-a-positive-trend-more-summer-sessions/60577.

Kelderman, Eric. 2012. "Tying Lawmakers' Hands in Calif." *Chronicle of Higher Education* (August 13). http://www.chronicle.com/article/Tying-Lawmakers-Hands-in/133571.

Keller, Josh. 2009a. "At Transfer Time, Thousands of California Students Hit a Dead End." *Chronicle of Higher Education* (October 5). http://www.chronicle.com/article/At-Transfer-Time-Thousands-of/48678.

Keller, Josh. 2009b. "California Community Colleges May Reduce Enrollment by 250,000." *Chronicle of Higher Education* (May 21). http://www.chronicle.com/article/California-Community-Colleges/117230.

Keller, Josh. 2009c. "California's Public Universities to Cut Salaries and Enrollment in Budget Crunch." *Chronicle of Higher Education* (July 10). http://www.chronicle.com/article/Californias-Public/47867.

Keller, Josh. 2009d. "Cal State Campuses Are Forced to Reject Thousands." *Chronicle of Higher Education* (April 10). http://www.chronicle.com/article/Cal-State-Campuses-Are-Forced/32514.

Keller, Josh. 2011. "Facing New Cuts, California's Colleges Are Shrinking Their Enrollments." *Chronicle of Higher Education* (January 13). http://www.chronicle.com/article/Facing-New-Cuts-Californias/125945.

"Published and Net Tuition Fees, by Sector, 1993–94 to 2013–14." 2014. *Chronicle of Higher Education* (August 18). http://www.chronicle.com/article/PublishedNet-Tuition/147513.

Quintana, Chris, and Joshua Hatch. 2017. "177 Private Colleges Fail Education Dept.'s Financial-Responsibility Test." *Chronicle of Higher Education* (March 8). http://www.chronicle.com/article/177-Private-Colleges-Fail/239436.

"Rankings." 2017. https://woodbury.edu/about/about-woodbury/about-woodbury-2/.

Repko, Allen, Rich Szostak, and Michelle Phillips Buchberger. 2013. *Introduction to Interdisciplinary Studies.* Thousand Oaks, CA: Sage.

Western Association of Schools and Colleges (WASC) Visiting Team. 2010. "Report of the WASC Visiting Team Educational Effectiveness Review: Woodbury University." Unpublished report, March 8–10.

Woodbury University Intuitional Research. 2017. "RE: Institutional Demographics." E-mail message to author, May 18.

Woodbury University Writing Department. 2017. "WRIT Enrollment Report." *PowerCampus by Ellucian,* May 18.

Yancey, Kathleen Blake. 2004. "Made Not Only in Words: Composition in a New Key." *College Composition and Communication* 56 (2): 297–328.

7

DRAWING NEW LESSONS FROM OLD STORIES
How Economic Arguments Re-Shaped the Values of a Newly Independent Writing Program

Jamie White-Farnham

The field of rhetoric and composition in the United States since the nineteenth century has often concerned itself with the connections among money, employment, social class, and the teaching of writing. Take, for example, three well-known origin stories of the discipline that illustrate this claim:

The first origin story I learned, probably because I attended a land-grant university, begins with the 1862 Morrill Land-Grant Act, which called for the designation of public land and money to establish state universities in part to "promote the liberal and practical education of the industrial classes in the several pursuits and professions in life" (National Archives 1862). Once the universities were established, students from working-class and agricultural families, now able to afford and attend college, did not have the capacity of language to express themselves in prose in ways that met their professors' expectations, necessitating freshman courses in writing (Sawyer 2009, 71).

Another story is told about the beginnings of writing classes at Harvard in 1874. According to James Berlin (1987, 20), "Charles William Eliot, Harvard's president from 1869–1909, had in fact considered writing so central to the new elective curriculum he was shaping that in 1874 the freshman English course at Harvard was established [and] by 1897 was the only required course in the curriculum." Attendant to the creation of the courses was the practice of entrance exams, which, according to Berlin (1987, 23), "ensured that the new open university would not become too open, allowing the new immigrants, for example, to earn degrees in science or mathematics without demonstrating by their use of language that they belonged in the middle class."

DOI: 10.7330/9781607328957.c007

A final origin story, that of the well-known beginnings of basic writing in 1970 by Mina Shaughnessy, also springs from the tension between working-class persons' language use and university expectations. Shaughnessy championed students' abilities even when their preparation and experience with language challenged ideas about who could and couldn't succeed in the university (Maher 1997, 114). Jane Maher credits Shaughnessy with the activism and view toward linguistic democracy that is more widely embraced today.

I begin with these origin stories because they highlight the ways teachers and scholars of writing have disagreed over the extent to which they should ignore or embrace the financial and social realities of their students. Shaughnessy in particular called attention to the ways traditional "expectations" ignored and marginalized whole swaths of the student population. What these stories illustrate to me is not necessarily the overcoming of the elitism and racism that underlie historical decisions about how to teach writing; instead, they remind me that prevarication in regard to how economics and writing education affect each other is still at work today, even if not in the blatantly elitist and racist forms of the past.

I say this as a member of an independent writing program that did little explicitly to acknowledge or enhance students' economic expectations of their college degrees until our own financial stability was threatened during and after the recession. As many of our middle-class forebears demonstrate in these stories, our program's teaching, beliefs about, and use of language betrayed our material comfort. Once that comfort was shaken, our program, in order to flourish, began to open its attitude about the purpose of teaching writing, which had been unconsciously entrenched in a belle-lettres paradigm that values beauty and imagination to the exclusion of other values. The new attitude includes practical and economic values besides.

This chapter, then, explains how the Writing Program at the University of Wisconsin–Superior seized *kairotic* moments during financial uncertainty to make arguments on behalf of our existence, centered around the economic value of writing education, something we had not previously entertained in any strategic way. In creating these arguments, we eventually reevaluated the purpose and value of our curriculum, making changes that have helped our program grow while others in similar conditions have foundered. I suggest that this is the result of a release of what Mary Sue Garay (1988, 5) once termed the "filthy lucre complex," or an unwillingness to acknowledge the economic implications of education and literacy and which, tacitly or not, had a hold on our perceptions of ourselves as writers and teachers of writing.

SETTING THE STAGE FOR INDEPENDENCE

The University of Wisconsin–Superior (UW-Superior), a small, public liberal arts college on the westernmost tip of Lake Superior, was established as Superior Normal School in 1893 in a rash of expansions to teacher education in the growing state of Wisconsin. The city of Superior and its counterpart across the St. Louis River, Duluth, Minnesota, are known as the Twin Ports. Over the years, Superior Normal School evolved into Superior State University and eventually, as did all of Wisconsin's state colleges, became part of the UW System in 1971.

Like its sister campuses, UW-Superior faced economic and political challenges in the aftermath of some extreme measures taken by a conservative governor in 2015, including a 30 percent state funding decrease; a tuition freeze; an attempt to change the mission of the University of Wisconsin, editing its founding philosophy of "the Wisconsin Idea" and replacing it with a focus on job creation (Herzog 2015); and, most recently, the "gutting" of the concept of tenure in the system (Flaherty 2016).

Despite the harsh conditions that posed a significant threat to other UW campuses' standing, including its flagship campus in Madison (Herzog and Gallagher 2016), UW-Superior, as the saying goes, had nearly nothing left to lose. Preexisting problems since the recession such as dwindling enrollment and a previous tuition freeze had already caused campus administrators to make unpopular decisions by 2011, such as canceling community-oriented programs, outsourcing the bookstore and the janitorial staff, and cutting some smaller programs such as several masters degrees (Associated Press 2015).

Perhaps unsurprisingly, the loss of enrollments was felt *after* a spike in enrollment seemingly inspired by the recession. As a result of layoffs, community members sought new training and education to change careers or improve their employability. UW-Superior saw a high in enrollments with 2,865 students in 2010, which has not again been reached (Institutional Research University of Wisconsin–Superior 2010). Since then, the coinciding tuition freeze and continued lack of state support set the scene for the curricular changes that will be described presently.

Coming out of the recession, the decline in enrollments offered the first whiff of needed financial streamlining. A first measure taken by the provost was the restructuring of academic departments to cut down on support staff and maximize the release time from teaching given to department chairs (one–two classes, depending on the size of the department).

The Writing Program, as a thread of the English department, had experienced some of the typical tensions the reader might imagine, including a minority of writing faculty and an overreliance on adjuncts to teach first-year and basic writing. However, there also existed a hopeful contingent of faculty who had created a writing minor in 2009. The minor was a loose connection of creative writing courses and upper-level rhetoric seminars. Still, despite some interesting work and excited students, the writing faculty was stuck in a second-class position, both in terms of personnel and the esteem of their curriculum by English colleagues, who prioritized the analysis of literature.

But part of the 2009 administrative realignment of departments included separating the Writing Program from the English Department and joining it with library science. Meanwhile, English joined foreign languages and English education. While library science and writing have found ways for their coexistence to have more meaning than a simple administrative arrangement (especially in the area of information literacy), the Writing Program and its curriculum was suddenly independent.

CHANGE THE FIRST: WRITING MAJOR

Inspired by the growing number of scholarly accounts of the creation of writing majors across the United States (see, for instance, Giberson, Nugent, and Ostergaard 2015), local evidence grew to suggest that a writing major might be successful. For one thing, the writing minor had grown to about forty students, two times larger than most humanities majors on our small campus. Drawing on our curricular strengths and making interdisciplinary connections with other departments such as psychology, anthropology, and legal studies to offer a variety of electives, the major delivers outcomes related to our university's liberal arts–inspired learning goals: communication, individual and social responsibility, and critical and creative thinking. Some additions were needed to satisfy graduation requirements on our campus, such as a senior capstone course for students to prepare professional-quality e-portfolios, as well as an internship course to facilitate students' experiences with area businesses and organizations.

The road to proposing this major was not bump-free; in fact, we faced opposition from colleagues who seemed to resent our efforts to grow during a time of cuts. However, a *kairotic* moment presented itself when the university hired an outside consultant to conduct research into employment opportunities in relation to each program on campus. Administration imagined that once faculty knew of employment trends in the region, they might readjust their curriculum to suit the data. The consultant's report was unwelcome to many. For instance, some faculty who had their ears to the ground in their own industries knew local information about upcoming retirements or personnel changes that could not be accounted for in the consultant's survey; therefore, some of the information was discredited. Further, other faculty found themselves staring at data that indicated there were no jobs for their graduates. In these cases, some rightly pointed out that if the consultant expected job openings to be labeled things like "history" or "philosophy," then the research was never legitimate in the first place.

The results for "writing" were just as broad and, at a different time, would have been less welcome to the Writing Program faculty. The report showed potential job growth in technical writing, an area we had no expertise in. Still, we seized on it; there is potential job growth in writing. These findings gave us evidence our administrators had already bought into to make our case. The shorthand name of this consulting firm and their report, ClearStream (a pseudonym), became our rally cry and enthymeme. I am not exaggerating when I say that sometimes, when explaining or defending our proposal, we could simply say "well, you know, ClearStream," and be understood by an audience nodding their heads.

In a different, less financially stressed context, our argument would have centered around the liberal arts values and practices we share with our campus colleagues, such as critical reading, clear and flexible communication skills, and an awareness of the world. These were, of course, still a part of the argument. However, given that financial straits were the key concern of administrators, our argument took on an emphatic arrangement, with the economic value of the writing major becoming the most important reason for its approval: writing is a job, students will get these jobs, and we will graduate more students if they know their major will lead to a job.

We are in the fifth year of this major. We are ranked, still, as a very large minor for humanities (about forty) and an average number of majors (about twenty). Some of the financial fervor has died down on campus, but we continue to operate and promote the major by way of its economic value. For example, we've established some internships, including one in technical writing at a major regional power company, and we've created a Community Advisory Board of local professionals to review and provide suggestions on our curriculum. These advisers hail from government, industry, and the more artistic side of the field, including publishers and editors of regional presses.

CHANGE THE SECOND: CORE WRITING COURSES

The biggest piece of our independent writing program is composed of the "core" writing courses in the general education curriculum: two first-year writing courses in a 101/102 sequence. This is a piece shared by all of our instructors: our permanent faculty who teach in the major/minor, our full-time instructors, and a devoted core of adjunct instructors. Each semester, about fifteen people teach about sixty sections of the two courses. It is a traditional arrangement: Writing 101 in the fall, Writing 102 in the spring. It has existed for probably more than forty years without real inspection or change.

Curiously, however, as we began to focus on the economic value of our new writing major, we also realized that we had perhaps given short shrift to a main practical goal of our university: to graduate employable people. Garay (1988, 5) explains this unexamined belief well: "The bias against the work world [the filthy lucre complex] is the byproduct of many beliefs that we English professionals hold about ourselves, our subject, and our profession . . . After all, won't the analytical writing skills we teach during literature lessons transfer to the workplace?" Our program had also accepted a similar loose understanding of and belief in "transfer" of the writing knowledge and skills in our curriculum. In addition, the courses' only foundational philosophy was a mix of the tradition of their existence and a general affinity for belle lettres, the literary and rhetorical tradition that both prizes, and is critiqued for, its preoccupation with beauty, clarity, and grace.

Realizing this error of omission, the twin pillars of the mission of our university—intellectual growth and career preparation—prompted our thinking about revising the core writing courses. Our courses focused on traditional academic writing skills such as critical reading, writing process, information literacy, and argument *twice*, in both of the first-year classes. We came to believe that the loose, implied link between academic writing and students' future work was a weakness, and we were motivated to strike a balance between the two halves of the mission.

Another year, another bumpy road. This time, our colleagues expressed worry and sometimes anger about ending a long curricular tradition. Again, ClearStream was a key piece of our argument, but, closer to home, the aforementioned university mission—intellectual growth and career preparation—led the way. Our proposal was approved after a protracted debate. While there are still two core courses, they are split between the first two years of the students' college experience: students take Introduction to Academic Writing in their first year and Introduction to Professional Writing in the second. In two years of implementation, we can report that the change happened relatively smoothly, and we look forward to reflecting more fully in a few years' time.

CONCLUSION

As a writing program administrator, I find the truly rhetorical nature of these changes notable. It is probably not a shock that a writing program moved quickly, took advantage of a timely opportunity, or made convincing arguments. But I believe that in cushier circumstances, our pace would have been slower, and our values would have stayed static. Most notably, our independence occasioned the consideration of which purposes and philosophies were assumed and desirable on the part of our curriculum in the first place. Had I been asked to develop an ideal writing major or core curriculum in a vacuum, what I would have conceived would look quite different. In reality, our circumstances forged our arguments, tactics, and decisions. Because of that, we expanded our perspective on the value of a writing education, arguing hardest of all to require a course in professional writing under the premise of its economic benefit to all students.

Thinking about the most serious moments of financial crisis on our campus—when protestors marched to try and keep the janitors employed, and when shouting matches occurred over the loss of all but one foreign language—the origin stories of our field remind me that economic and social conditions, not only of our students but of our institutions, have always affected what and how we teach. In the nineteenth century, institutions had the edge on students and functioned in part as a gatekeeper to prosperity. In the twentieth century, that function was challenged.

In the twenty-first century, it seems neither institutions nor students gain an advantage. Our governments' attitudes toward and funding of institutions of higher education are in decline. Worse still, the economy of higher education extends to students as many obstacles as opportunities to economic prosperity. These are conditions in which it is difficult to find footing. In the original story of the independent writing program described here, our first step was to consider an old and complicated aspect of writing education in a new and difficult context. We (re)learned that concern for economic prosperity and high-quality writing education are not mutually exclusive; they are indeed coterminous.

REFLECTION

Our coeditors note that complications arise around the definition and value of "independence" for writing programs. One complication of our independence was that it belied the good reasons a program should embrace healthy, mutual dependence with its counterparts across the university. This truth became clear to me during the debate over our core courses: *writing belongs to the university*. At first, I was indignant: what do *they* know? Writing is *our* discipline. It was an immature attitude; however, WPAs are steeped in the mind-set that disciplinarity is good and independence is best. The desire to break away from English had instilled the idea that *any* other discipline was a threat to our growth.

Now, with these experiences behind me, I accept that writing belongs to the university in material and philosophical senses. Materially speaking, our program can only exist in its context—a university that remains underfunded and under-enrolled. As exciting as our story is, the others in this book attest to the boom-and-bust cycle of writing and rhetoric majors that I should not ignore. Realistically, our core courses will remain our bread and butter. With that said, philosophically, I have come to appreciate the fact that writing belongs to the university via its capacity for transdisciplinarity—or participating in the larger political project of public higher education in creative ways alongside other disciplines. Where I was once frustrated with writing's place at the "bottom" of the curriculum, I now value its role as one of many disciplinary roots.

REFERENCES

Associated Press. 2015. "UW-Superior Cuts Nearly Half of Graduate Programs as Deficit Looms." *Milwaukee Journal Sentinel*, May 24. http://archive.jsonline.com/news/education/uw-superior-cuts-grad-programs-as-deficit-looms-b99277373z1–260535791.html.

Berlin, James. 1987. *Rhetoric and Reality: Writing Instruction in American College, 1900–1985*. Carbondale: Southern Illinois University Press.

Flaherty, Colleen. 2016. "What Remains of Tenure." *Inside Higher Education*, December 7. https://www.insidehighered.com/news/2016/12/07/faculty-members-university-wisconsin-oppose-proposed-change-new-post-tenure-review.

Garay, Mary Sue. 1988. "On Work and English." In *Expanding Literacies: English Teaching and the New Workplace*, ed. Mary Sue Garay and Stephen A. Bernhard, 3–20. Albany: State University of New York Press.

Giberson, Gregory A., Jim Nugent, and Lori A. Ostergaard, eds. 2015. *Writing Majors: Eighteen Program Profiles*. Logan: Utah State University Press.

Herzog, Karen. 2015. "Walker Proposes Changing Wisconsin Idea—Then Backs Away." *Milwaukee Journal Sentinel*, February 4. http://archive.jsonline.com/news/education/scott-walkers-uw-mission-rewrite-could-end-the-wisconsin-idea-b99439020z1-290797681.html.

Herzog, Karen, and Kathleen Gallagher. 2016. "UW-Madison Says State Cuts Threaten Research Stature." *Milwaukee Journal Sentinel*, December 18. http://www.jsonline.com/story/news/education/2016/12/18/uw-madison-say-state-cuts-threaten-research-stature/94605990.

Institutional Research University of Wisconsin–Superior. 2010. "Common Data Set 2010." *UW-Superior Fact Book*. Superior: University of Wisconsin–Superior.

Maher, Jane. 1997. *Mina Shaughnessy: Her Life and Work*. Urbana, IL: National Council for English Education.

National Archives and Records Administration. 1862. "Transcript of the Morill Act." *Our Documents*. https://www.ourdocuments.gov/doc.php?flash=true&doc=33&page=transcript.

Sawyer, Paul. 2009. "The Writing Program and the Call to Service." *Michigan Journal of Community Service Learning* 15 (2): 68–76.

PART II

Adjusting Existing Curricula in Response to the Great Recession

8
SURVIVING AND THRIVING IN THE WRITING DEPARTMENT AT LOYOLA UNIVERSITY MARYLAND

Cindy Moore and Peggy O'Neill

DEPARTMENT PROFILE

For decades, writing has been housed separately from English at Loyola, in variously configured programs and then departments—the Communication Arts Program (1972–77), the Writing Program (1977–83), the Writing Department (1983–85), the Writing and Media Department (1986–99), the Communication Department (1999–2004), and finally back to the Writing Department (2004–present). While most of our current faculty earned their degrees from traditional English departments, on the whole, we identify less as literary scholars and more as writers of all types of literary and non-literary texts, from poems and short stories to essays, articles, and academic books. Our sheer longevity, combined with our collective writerly identity, makes it unlikely that a money-conscious administrator would consider merging us with another department at all, let alone the English Department, which has forged its own identity around literary history, theory, and analysis. In fact, given the challenges facing liberal arts institutions like Loyola, and in light of the many nationally publicized recommendations for meeting those challenges, our independent writing department (IWD) is in a position to continue to grow and thrive and to help our institution attract talented students. In an increasingly competitive higher education marketplace, the Writing Department could easily be promoted as a distinguishing feature of our institution, since many of our closest competitors do not have independent writing departments.

The Loyola Writing Department offers a BA in writing, with a curriculum constructed to provide majors with a basic foundation in poetry, fiction, literary nonfiction, and rhetoric in addition to advanced coursework in those sub-fields, as well as areas such as professional writing, technical writing, screenwriting, science/environmental writing, and

DOI: 10.7330/9781607328957.c008

travel writing (see O'Neill and Mallonee 2015 for a fuller discussion of the development of the writing curriculum). Writing majors can elect to take all their eleven required courses within the department, or they can split coursework with another academic department (e.g., biology, communication, English, history, psychology) through our popular interdisciplinary major option. We also offer a six-course writing minor. At the core of this curriculum, and at the heart of our department, is the first-year writing course required of all Loyola students and taught by all faculty members. This one-semester course is focused on the essay, broadly defined. In it, students develop the creative and critical abilities necessary to communicate effectively in a range of writing contexts as they compose a variety of nonfiction texts including personal essays, profiles, op-eds, analyses, and articles. Though students engage in research to discover and develop what they want to say to their readers, the course is not an academic writing course per se; nor does it function as a traditional "service" course. We frame it as an introduction to what it means to be a writer within and outside of academe.

The department's efforts to nurture writers across campus have been enhanced throughout its history by participation in numerous university-wide initiatives and programs. From 1980 through the early 1990s, the department played a key role in a vibrant writing across the curriculum program funded by a National Endowment for the Humanities grant that supported not only faculty development but also faculty research (Mallonee and Breihan 1985; McCarthy 1987; Walvoord 1982; Walvoord and McCarthy 1990). Though this program, like so many others across the country, eventually dissolved from lack of consistent funding, remnants of it remain today, most noticeably in the cross-curricular work of the Loyola Writing Center, a department-based program. In addition, since the department's inception, writing faculty have been involved as administrators or instructors in almost every cross-campus undergraduate initiative the university has embraced, including the Honors Program, a diversity-course initiative, a first-year seminar program, a first-year living and learning program that replaced the original seminars, service learning, and study abroad (through a targeted online travel writing course). Writing faculty also initiated a creative writing/reading series that has brought students and faculty across campus together for over thirty years to listen to both prominent and emerging poets, fiction writers, and essayists from across the country (and occasionally from around the world). The department supports cocurricular activities such as a student-run literary magazine; a poetry "collective," which sponsors workshops and readings for aspiring poets;

a national writing honor society, Pi Epsilon Pi, that we founded in 2006; and a student club affiliated with the Rhetoric Society of America.

Our tenure-line faculty numbers twelve (seven hired since the 2008 recession), putting us on par with our peer departments in the humanities. In addition, we currently have five, full-time, non-tenure-track instructors, supplemented by one to four per-course adjuncts, depending on the needs for that semester. Though most of us identify as specialists in a particular field, as a whole we are versatile, with degrees, publications, and teaching experience that cross sub-areas and genres. The breadth of our individual backgrounds equips many of us to design and teach courses across our departmental curriculum.

Recently, we moved into a new, renovated department space, in which faculty offices, a department seminar room, a student lounge, and the writing center are located on a single floor near academic advising, first-year programming, and the School of Business. This move away from most of the humanities departments, including English, enhanced our sense of departmental identity and increased our visibility on campus. Prior to the move, students often had trouble finding the department, tucked away as it was in a corner of a renovated Tudor mansion. And because we were across the hall from the English Department suite, students and faculty peers frequently considered us all one department, in spite of our long history of being two distinct units. The previous writing center was also hard to find in its location in the basement of a university administrative building, separated from the department. Now, both the department and the writing center are designated stops on campus tours for new and prospective students. Our hallway—filled with display cabinets and both traditional and digital bulletin boards—showcases faculty publications, promotes student work, and educates the many people passing through about what we offer as a department.

CHALLENGES, OLD AND NEW

Despite being well-established at Loyola, the Writing Department has faced several challenges, both recent and long-standing. Like other humanities departments, for example, we saw our enrollments dip considerably after the recession. Though our numbers have been increasing over the past several years, the faculty resources we have had to devote to recruitment are considerable. Beyond difficulties convincing anxious parents and students that writing is indeed a viable major for a successful career, we experienced a number of internal changes that complicated recruitment efforts. Several long-term faculty members, many of them popular with students, retired or left the university. Though, as noted above, we have been able to add seven tenure-line faculty members, the relatively short time frame for hiring (e.g., six new assistant professors in five years) required the five senior faculty members to turn much of their attention away from activities like student recruitment toward hiring and mentoring junior faculty. Finally, while senior faculty led a substantial revision of our major curriculum in 2009–10, with the goal of expanding rhetoric and professional writing options that would attract more and more-diverse students in the long run, the changes, which included a required introductory rhetoric course, may have discouraged the traditional creative writing students. Changes in university-wide programming also affected long-standing recruitment mechanisms. The implementation of a new university first-year living-learning program, for instance, forced us to eliminate a once-popular departmental by-invitation first-year seminar program that had been a vital recruiting tool. In addition, the Honors Program, which had been a steady source of writing majors and minors, changed so drastically that our faculty who had long taught in Honors could no longer easily see how they might contribute to the new curriculum.

Other challenges we have faced as an independent department are less unique to Loyola and more a matter of public perceptions, graduate-school professionalization, and, related to that, traditional higher education structures that are difficult to shift. Beyond the usual recruitment problems humanities departments often experience during economic downturns, for example, IWDs often have trouble explaining how the learning opportunities available in a writing department differ from those offered in an English or communication department. While distinguishing departments through lists of courses may be relatively easy (e.g., at Loyola, the English Department offers only literature courses; the Communication Department offers news writing, broadcasting, and advertising courses), the historical overlap among disciplines makes clear demarcations difficult. All three departments at Loyola emphasize writing and infuse writing throughout their curricula; all prioritize helping students develop strong critical reading and thinking abilities. While faculty can reason with each other that writing and communication focus more on textual production of various types and English more on schools of textual interpretation, this distinction often seems lost on prospective students and families. Similarly, the ultimate blurriness of boundaries between "creative" and "critical" writing makes it difficult to articulate how a course in travel writing offered by the Writing Department might differ from a communication course in travel reporting. And in some ways the distinctions, though possibly helpful for recruitment, are not so helpful with respect to what we know from our theories and research about how genres really function.

In the end, as a department, we try to articulate for ourselves and others our unique perspective on writing and teaching (i.e., that writing is a complex individual and social knowledge-making process, requiring "continued practice and informed guidance"; Council of Writing Program Administrators 2014). We have found that our biggest selling points, beyond the ability to study various genres of writing, are the interdisciplinary major (which can combine with nearly any academic major on campus), the writing minor (which can enhance any transcript), our many extra-curricular activities, our internship program, and the opportunity to prepare for, and work in, a university writing center.

Though, unlike some other IWDs, we have not had to struggle much to convince two different deans to support new tenure-line hires, we have struggled to attract and hire the right faculty. Because most prospective hires are professionalized in traditional English departments, they are often unfamiliar with the idea, let alone the reality, of an IWD. Further, the way graduate students are trained to specialize in one area, often to the exclusion of other areas, does not help our efforts to attract truly intradisciplinary candidates. We find that the candidates who fit our curricular needs best are those who did cross-disciplinary work in graduate school (e.g., the fiction writer who also took graduate courses in composition and rhetorical theory), or those who have degrees in both creative writing and composition and rhetoric, or perhaps the poet who developed expertise in literary nonfiction. A further challenge for us is attracting faculty who can teach an essay-based first-year composition course, which is an introduction to our vertical curriculum and taught by all departmental faculty. Most applicants for positions in our department have taught first-year courses that are centered on academic argument, academic research writing, or both. Though our course includes attention to argument and research, students write essays of various types for many different purposes and audiences, only some of which would require academic research cited in an academic style.

Finally, while fiscal concerns have not hindered our ability to expand our faculty or our space, they have impacted our capacity to offer the number and variety of courses needed to attract majors and minors back to the department. Through 2010, we were still able to offer low-enrolled specialty courses that allowed small cohorts of students to advance in a particular area (e.g., poetry). Over the past few years, as Loyola, like other private liberal arts schools, has struggled to maintain quality programs without being able to raise tuition, we have been asked to limit course offerings that attract fewer than ten students. So, as we try to build a relatively new professional writing program that includes science writing courses, or to support an always small but passionate number of promising poets, we find ourselves having to offer new or traditionally important courses less frequently (or sometimes canceling them), which, then, negatively affects recruitment or frustrates declared majors.

Recruitment-minded curricular planning has been further complicated by a post-recession feeling among students that they not only must graduate in four years but must pack more and more into those years in an effort to look attractive to employers. Double majors with double minors, multiple internships, service learning courses, and study abroad—all of this puts pressure on our upper-level curriculum. For example, because undergraduate writing courses are uniquely American (and to some degree British), writing majors who study abroad have a difficult time finding courses that count for our major (which is the reason we offer an online travel writing course). The university's large core curriculum, which requires students to take a specific number of courses in each of five humanities departments, meet a two-year foreign language requirement, and take additional coursework in science and social science, means that students have very few, if any, electives and are often reluctant to "spend" one on a writing course that might interest them but may seem unrelated to their chosen major or not "fun." This reluctance especially affects our ability to attract business, education, and science majors, whose degree program requirements are particularly numerous, restricting elective options even further.

AMID THE CHALLENGES, A PROMISING FUTURE

In spite of these challenges, our department is on solid ground and moving forward, as the university's commitment to new tenure-line hires and an expansive new space suggests. As our faculty has stabilized, we have been able to reinvigorate our recruiting efforts, for example, by identifying and inviting first-year students to take more writing classes, organizing alumni panels to help students understand how writing majors and minors transition to the work world, and initiating a new speaker series, "Writers at Work," that invites practicing editors and writers to campus to talk about careers in these areas. These efforts along with enhanced collaboration with undergraduate admissions to highlight our programs—are paying off, with more incoming students indicating writing as a potential major.

Within a higher education context that is beginning to recognize both the enhanced learning possibilities and fiscal efficiencies of cross-disciplinary work, and a new university strategic plan that calls for "integral synergies" and "interdisciplinary connections" across academic divisions (Loyola University Maryland n.d.), our department is well positioned to help Loyola move in this direction. Given our history of working with faculty across campus through our interdisciplinary major, the writing center, service learning, and interdisciplinary minors (i.e., film studies, gender studies), we have found it easy to partner with colleagues across campus to support the first-year interdisciplinary living-learning program as well as new initiatives. For example, we are participating in two new interdisciplinary minors—environmental and sustainability studies and peace and justice studies—which seems to be helping us recruit students to some of our upper-level courses. Writing faculty have also been involved in interdisciplinary grant applications, one related to environmental studies and one focused on teaching technical writing for engineering students. As our junior faculty earn—or make progress toward—tenure and promotion, they are better able to see how they might participate in cross-disciplinary efforts, including those that seemed closed off to writing faculty just a few years ago. For example, two newer faculty (one recently tenured and one at the midway point) designed a rhetoric course that would work for the revised university Honors Program, allowing the department to once again enjoy a presence there.

While our interdisciplinary inclinations make it possible for us to imagine an important role for ourselves at a university that is starting to appreciate the potential of cross-disciplinary work, ultimately, we believe, as Kurt Spellmeyer (2002, 287, 279) does, that our future, the future of Loyola, and indeed the future of higher education lie in our ability to challenge the very notion of disciplinarity, especially as it is based on "philosophic or ideological truth." Instead, we can consider how we, as writing specialists, might work to help our colleagues "make visible" to themselves and others the knowledge they can offer students that is of real "consequence" to them and the increasingly complex world in which they live. This perspective, along with our successful history of working across the disciplines, will be especially useful during the reimagining of the undergraduate curriculum, including both general education and major requirements Loyola has recently undertaken. It is not insignificant, we think, that in addition to reaffirming our first-year composition course as an essential component of a revised curriculum, all of the curricular proposals now under consideration include an interdisciplinary component, whether it be an upper-level gen-ed course that might be taught from a variety of disciplinary perspectives or a required cross-disciplinary "cluster" of courses. Instead of worrying about our department or its offerings being cut, writing faculty members at Loyola are in the fortunate position of being able to imagine new and exciting opportunities for themselves and their students.

REFLECTION

As we have further revised this chapter and our university continues to face the challenges associated with the changing context of higher education, we continue to find strength in our intradisciplinary department identity. Student interest in cross-curricular connections remains high, as demonstrated by increasing numbers of interdisciplinary writing majors and writing minors, and by increasing numbers of interdisciplinary and multidisciplinary initiatives across campus that writing faculty support. While our challenges have remained, one factor that has changed is that the anticipated radical revision of the university's undergraduate curriculum has stalled. Given the uncertainty about how writing will figure into a future general education—or "core"—curriculum, we will need to be proactive about attracting students to our courses and working across campus with our peers in other departments to ensure that Loyola students are prepared for the writing demands of the twenty-first century.

REFERENCES

Council of Writing Program Administrators. 2014. "WPA Outcomes Statement for First-Year Composition (v3.0)." http://wpacouncil.org/positions/outcomes.html.

Loyola University Maryland. n.d. "The Ignatian Compass: Strategic Plan 2017–2022." http://www.loyola.edu/about/strategic-plan.

Mallonee, Barbara C., and John R. Breihan. 1985. "Responding to Students' Drafts: Interdisciplinary Consensus." *College Composition and Communication* 36: 213–31.

McCarthy, Lucille P. 1987. "A Stranger in Strange Lands: A College Student Writing across the Curriculum." *Research in the Teaching of English* 21: 233–65.

O'Neill, Peggy, and Barbara Mallonee. 2015. "Reforming and Transforming Writing in the Liberal Arts Context: The Writing Department at Loyola University Maryland." In *Writing Majors: Eighteen Program Profiles*, ed. Greg Giberson, Jim Nugent, and Lori Ostergaard, 47–60. Logan: Utah State University Press.

Spellmeyer, Kurt. 2002. "Bigger Than a Discipline?" In *Field of Dreams: Independent Writing Programs and the Future of Composition Studies*, ed. Peggy O'Neill, Angela Crow, and Larry Burton, 278–94. Logan: Utah State University Press.

Walvoord, Barbara E. Fassler. 1982. *Helping Students Write Well: A Guide for Teachers in All Disciplines*. New York: Modern Language Association.

Walvoord, Barbara E. Fassler, and Lucille P. McCarthy. 1990. *Thinking and Writing in College: A Naturalistic Study of Students in Four Disciplines*. Urbana, IL: National Council of Teachers of English.

9

THRIVING THROUGH DISRUPTION
Leveraging Alumni Experience to Support a Liberal Arts Writing Major

Amy Clements, Drew M. Loewe, and Mary Rist

Graduates in writing and rhetoric are entering a field that now experiences frequent disruption. Seismic shifts in modes of disseminating and receiving news, a rapidly evolving self-publishing landscape for creative writers, and the fluctuating economic tides of academia mean that what has worked in the past may not work in the future. Mutually beneficial communication with alumni, as well as regular curricular revision that revitalizes traditional rhetorical theory and criticism for new technologies, can help a writing program remain relevant and strong. Crucially, communication with alumni and professional preparation of students must be supported by the program and the institution itself through academic- and teaching-load credit and service recognition. By mitigating disruption by outside forces through activities such as these, a writing major can survive or even thrive, as ours has for three decades.

WHERE WE WERE

St. Edward's University, founded in 1885, is a Holy Cross–affiliated liberal arts university in Austin, Texas. St. Edward's has about 4,600 students, mostly traditional undergraduates. The university offers seven masters programs and, until recently, offered nontraditional older students a degree-completion program called New College. The writing and rhetoric major at St. Edward's has evolved over a long history that began in 1975, when a structural change to the traditional literature-focused English major was approved. As a result of that change, students could pursue an "emphasis" in writing studies. By 1982, and in response to student demand, the English major developed a larger writing studies "concentration." By 1987, the major had matured fully,

DOI: 10.7330/9781607328957.c009

becoming a standalone undergraduate degree program with its own prefix (ENGW–English Writing and Rhetoric).

Since the standalone major began, it has always had a core group of required courses. These courses have evolved over the years in an effort to remain relevant as new technologies, competencies, and theories of rhetoric have matured. The core courses were intended to create a rhetorical focus on the production of texts, not just the interpretation of texts; a focus on experiential learning; and a developmental structure of common experience for all writing majors, supplemented by electives that allowed for specialization. This arrangement worked well for a long time, and the writing major enjoyed strong enrollments, peaking in 2010 with 155 majors.

THE CRISIS HITS

The financial crisis of 2008 and later years affected all of higher education, including small private universities like St. Edward's. Our university is heavily tuition-dependent, but the national downturn in higher education exacerbated competition among private universities for strong students (who command tuition discounts) and curtailed corporate sponsorship of full-pay nontraditional students. Second, the university's Strategic Plan for 2015 (announced in 2010) prioritized "global understanding" as part of the university's Quality Enhancement Program that its accreditor, the Southern Association of Colleges and Schools Commission on Colleges (SACSCOC), requires. The university heavily recruited international students, enrolling students who often struggle with writing in English and are unlikely to enroll in an English writing major. The university also developed and heavily promoted programs in global studies and global business, adding to the internal competition for students that any university has. Finally, a smaller-than-expected tuition increase in 2014 created a gap of over $1 million between anticipated and actual tuition funds. The $1+ million gap—significant for a university of our size—spurred a comprehensive program of reexamining expenditures, the structure of academic units, and programs' continued relevance to the university mission. A new vice president for academic affairs was hired as part of this restructuring. Under her leadership, some programs were scaled back, and some senior faculty members were offered buyouts. As part of university-wide efforts to ensure continued relevance of curricula, the VPAA implemented a schedule for external program review and made the review a prerequisite for any faculty hiring.

REVAMPING THE CURRICULUM

Faced with declining enrollments, aware that parents and students were less likely to consider majors in the humanities as good investments, and cognizant of the ways digital media affected the practices and theories of writing and rhetoric, ENGW volunteered to be the first program in the School of Humanities to conduct a self-study and to invite external reviewers to campus. In fall 2014, three reviewers (Tim Peeples from Elon, Greg Giberson from Oakland University, and Carmen Jimenez from New Mexico State) came to campus. They met with faculty, students, and administrators. They wrote a report to the dean and VPAA that affirmed the self-study's call for curricular review and provided valuable suggestions.

Meetings during the spring and summer of 2015 were followed by a two-day faculty retreat in September 2015. Based on the results of the external report, as well as a university consultant's report, we were able to hire three new faculty members in spring 2015 to fill empty tenure-track lines. The new faculty provided invaluable assistance in the curriculum revision process, which culminated in a new curriculum and a new name for the major. Instead of being called English Writing and Rhetoric, ENGW, we would become Writing and Rhetoric, WRIT, a name we hoped would better distinguish us from our colleagues in the traditional English literature major and would better attract prospective students who saw themselves as writers. During the review process, we reached consensus on several key decisions.

Larger core with significant structure (versus smaller core with more flexibility): After extensive discussion and a review of various other models for core curricula, the faculty chose to remain a "hybrid major," a term Deborah Balzhiser and Susan McLeod (2010) used to refer to majors with elements of both liberal arts and professional preparation. This meant that despite administration calls for a smaller major (to allow for easy transfer from two-year institutions), we kept a large, albeit revised, required core (thirty credit hours). We retained but reimagined our courses in sentence craft and style while also retaining required courses in rhetorical criticism and history/theory. Our alumni often mentioned that both kinds of courses have proven helpful to them as they move forward in their careers. The new major also keeps the career preparation course and a required internship course as well as requiring an inquiry-based senior project.

Gateway courses: At the suggestion of our reviewers, we also re-envisioned how we introduce students to the major and to the various specializations in the major. Previously, our primary gateway course to the major had been an introductory linguistics course on English grammar. Wanting our students to have, as Janice Lauer (2003) suggests, a more "spacious" introductory understanding of what writing studies entails, we are designing Writing in the Digital Age, an introductory course to be taken concurrently with, or followed by, introductory courses in professional and creative writing. (After some prerequisites, students will also take a journalism and digital media course, meaning that all majors will have an introduction to all concentrations in the major.) In opting to require that all students take an introduction to creative writing workshop, faculty pointed to data suggesting that students who have taken such workshops are often more used to working collaboratively, using peer feedback constructively, and revising extensively. (At St. Edward's, creative writing courses have been prefixed as ENGW and taught by ENGL and ENGW faculty since the writing major split from the English major in the 1980s, so there were no turf battles to be fought there.) Faculty also pointed out that students needed an introduction to professional writing because they don't really know what "professional writing" means. Presenting the creative problem solving and storytelling involved in professional writing might help us retain self-identified "creative" writing majors who want to feel they are preparing for a profession that will excite and challenge them over the course of their careers.

Emphasis on multimodal composing and learning to learn new technologies: In the revised major, we recommitted ourselves to giving students a deep understanding of rhetoric and how it can help them use new technologies and address diverse communication situations throughout their professional careers. Our gateway course, Writing in the Digital Age, as well as the required journalism course, Digital Media Production and Design, advertise our intention to students. We want the major to help them develop flexible writing processes and to understand how they can harness the affordances of new media and new technologies effectively and rhetorically. Students create and design an e-portfolio of their work.

We also redesigned the specializations, renaming them "concentrations" to more accurately reflect the undergraduate nature of the courses. The professional writing concentration, in particular, was updated to offer courses in content management and social media.

TRACKING ALUMNI MORE CLOSELY

Through this revision process, we surveyed our current and former students, as well as area employers who supervised our student interns and often hired our graduates. The decision to keep a set of courses designed to help students become more versatile and rhetorically savvy editors was based in part on data from our alumni, who said those courses were among the most useful to them in their careers. Another aspect of the older curriculum that we chose to maintain was the intentional emphasis on career preparation. In fact, we have begun to formalize the ties between the internship in professional writing and our career preparation and alumni networking efforts.

Accurately tracking student outcomes after graduation proved to be imprecise and time-consuming work. Alumni may stay in contact with a professor after graduation, but faculty members must focus on their obligations to current students; systematically tracking students who have graduated isn't a priority. In contrast, university development officers and alumni outreach teams are challenged by the fact that they rarely have a personal connection to the graduates with whom they are attempting to build relationships.

To bridge this gap in our program, in 2015, a full-time, tenure-track faculty member was appointed by her chair to consolidate various duties related to students' professionalization, including alumni outreach, for the major. The usual teaching load for full-time faculty members at St. Edward's is twenty-four credit hours per academic year. Our alumni outreach coordinator was granted six hours of teaching-load credit per semester for teaching a required career preparation course, supervising professional writing internships, fostering connections with alumni, and maintaining a database that tracks careers and contact information of program graduates. All four of these functions are interrelated, and a system is now in place for our alumni to mentor and recruit current students as interns and as full-time hires while also serving as speakers in career preparation, providing current, real-world information on the expectations for writing and rhetoric majors, whether they aspire to immediately enter the workforce or pursue graduate studies. Both the career preparation course and the faculty-monitored internship are required of all our majors.

A comprehensive database of our program's alumni was finalized, listing the names of all 574 program graduates, beginning with the class of 1986. Corporate websites and social media (particularly LinkedIn and a Facebook group for our major) eased the fact-finding process, but outcomes and accurate contact information could not be discerned for all alumni. It was especially challenging to gather information on those who had graduated before 2000. Nonetheless, e-mail addresses were obtained for 406 alumni, and an IRB-approved survey was distributed to them with the primary aim of enhancing curriculum development activities. Delivering a response rate of 28 percent, 112 graduates completed the survey.

The survey questions reflected two essential areas of inquiry: How do our graduates fare professionally? How essential are creativity and adaptability to their success? The latter question arose not only from the previously mentioned data on the benefits of creative writing workshops but also from anecdotal comments made by multiple hiring managers when our curriculum revision process began. Representing the fields of advertising and technical writing, they recommended that a creative writing course in any genre be required of every writing and rhetoric major, and they stressed the importance of being able to revise in response to feedback from clients and colleagues.

One aspect of data collection was fraught with complexity. The survey included the question "Which categories best describe your current work?" and we permitted respondents to make more than one selection, choosing from fields we knew multiple alumni had entered. Our findings echoed the experience of researchers in the professional writing undergraduate major at Penn State Berks, whose 2009–10 alumni survey revealed that "respondents' job descriptions and duties did not fit into neat, preconceived categories, but were instead much more varied and wide-ranging than we had imagined" (Weisser and Grobman 2012, 48). We provided respondents with fourteen specific options, but the most commonly selected option was "other [specify]," which represented 20 percent of the responses.

The remaining top four responses were nonprofit work, digital marketing, and educator, which tied with social media marketing. By asking this question, we were able to cross-tabulate professions with responses to questions regarding creativity, internships, and involvement in extra-curricular activities. Nonetheless, our database already contained employment data on 411 alumni, which we coded using the categories offered in the survey. We determined that nonprofit workers may have been overrepresented in the survey, for they only comprise 6 percent of tracked alumni. Digital and social media marketing also appear to have been overrepresented, comprising only 8 percent and 1 percent of tracked alumni, respectively. Conversely, educators may have been underrepresented in the survey, as the database indicates that 17 percent of tracked alumni work in the field of education. These distinctions are reminders that surveys deliver information on respondents who are not necessarily representative of the surveyed population as a whole. That said, the "other" option jibed across both data collection methods, with 23 percent of tracked alumni classified in that category.

These highly varied employment data underscore the versatility of an undergraduate degree in writing. Our program has led hundreds of graduates to success in dozens of career paths that require strong writing, editing, and research skills but are rarely tied to the world of conventional publishing. In turn, respondents underscored the necessity of versatility on the job:

- 86 percent reported that creative thinking was always or often valued by their clients and colleagues
- 85 percent reported that being able to identify problems in a given situation and find good solutions to those problems is very important in their profession
- 77 percent reported that is it very important for them to be able to take criticism well and improve projects as a result of critique
- 70 percent reported that the ability to learn new knowledge and skills is very important in their profession.

In qualitative responses, a majority of alumni voiced appreciation for courses that delivered realistic assignments (with courses in grammar, editing, and technical writing named most frequently), along with courses that translated theoretical concepts into practical applications. Not surprisingly, when asked which skills we should emphasize more, digital literacy was the most common recommendation, ranging from "writing for digital media, specifically search engines and social media," to "digital storytelling/Creativist/Atavist."

Alumni of the program have, through their participation in surveys and their recruitment and mentoring of current students, proved to be an invaluable resource, one we had not fully appreciated before the department made a conscious effort at alumni outreach. Our institution has a dedicated Career Development Center and an Alumni Office, but departmental outreach is also crucial.

CONCLUSION

As an IWP separate from the literature program, we have built (and then rebuilt) a curriculum on rhetoric, on the study and practice of language and its use in multiple situations. Rhetoric, as its history has shown, is inherently interdisciplinary, with methods and theories that apply across many fields and integrate knowledge from different domains. Highlighting our connection to rhetoric rather than to literature has also positioned our IWP well among other areas of the university, making WRIT faculty valuable on writing across the curriculum (WAC) and writing in the disciplines (WID) initiatives and maintaining buy-in across campus for a two-semester general education writing requirement. In addition, in our particular case, given our long history as a major, when administrative convenience necessitated a merger with our literature colleagues into a department of literature, writing, and rhetoric, there was little conflict and no sense that the writing major (still a separate BA with more than double the majors of literature) would be forced to give up any of the disciplinary ground still being fought for by so many of the newer IWPs profiled by Greg Giberson, Jim Nugent, and Lori Ostergaard in their 2015 anthology.

Our WRIT alumni have recognized the power of language in their work and have acknowledged that understanding rhetorical concepts such as audience, genre, and *kairos* has helped them succeed in their professions. The WRIT curriculum has maintained its connection to rhetoric, and we remain committed to teaching rhetoric as an interdisciplinary liberal art, even as we have adapted the curriculum in postrecession years to better acknowledge digital means of production and to better frame the program as forward-moving and relevant preparation for professions. Feedback from our alumni provided important support for this move, and we continue to involve alumni in our program. Highlighting their success has proven rhetorically effective to a variety of stakeholders—and practically useful for our students—especially in post-recession years. Documenting career paths and graduate programs pursued by our alumni allows us to impress parents (and other funders) of the value of a BA in writing and rhetoric for students interested in creative or professional writing, journalism, or rhetorical theory.

Despite the disruption felt throughout the university and higher education at large after the recession, the IWP at St. Edward's has remained strong and even started to gradually rebound. Our numbers have already started to improve; in fall 2016, we had 104 majors. As we enter our fourth decade as an undergraduate writing major, we continue to look both inside and outside our program for ways to keep writing and rhetoric relevant and attractive to our current and prospective students.

REFLECTION

We might reflect with scholars of interdisciplinary studies that an IWP like ours with a curriculum built (and rebuilt) on rhetorical theory and practice is as inherently interdisciplinary as rhetoric itself. WRIT faculty have participated in WAC and WID initiatives and been at the forefront of working with other disciplines in updating general education writing courses. We have reframed "service" courses as valuable interdisciplinary explorations: digital marketing majors elect to take Writing in the Digital Age, political science students take Analyzing Rhetoric, video game development students and theater arts students take Playwriting and Writing for the Stage and Screen. We also have an interdisciplinary partnership with creative writing, which gives us a foot in the literary side of the house without being controlled by it and allows creative writing students to gain a rhetorical sensitivity for language and its effects in the world. Professional writing students study creativity and empathy building in workshop courses.

Promoting the interdisciplinary value of rhetoric may be a key to helping students address the wicked problems of the future, including how to analyze, use, and resist professional discourses and technological tools that change constantly. Interdisciplinarity may also allow our IWP to weather this and future storms in higher education, which is also in constant flux.

REFERENCES

Balzhiser, Deborah, and Susan McLeod. 2010. "The Undergraduate Writing Major: What Is It? What Should It Be?" *College Composition and Communication* 61 (3): 415–33.

Giberson, Greg, Jim Nugent, and Lori Ostergaard, eds. 2015. *Writing Majors: Eighteen Program Profiles.* Logan: Utah State University Press.

Lauer, Janice. "The Spaciousness of Rhetoric." 2003. In *Beyond Postprocess and Postmodernism: Essays on the Spaciousness of Rhetoric,* ed. Theresa Enos and Keith D. Miller, 3–16. Mahwah, NJ: Lawrence Erlbaum.

Weisser, Christian, and Laurie Grobman. 2012. "Undergraduate Writing Majors and the Rhetoric of Professionalism." *Composition Studies* 40 (1): 39–59.

10

CONTEXT, STRATEGY, IDENTITY
A History of Change in the UC Santa Barbara Writing Program

Madeleine Sorapure and Linda Adler-Kassner

To survive and thrive, independent writing programs must remain responsive to, and proactive within, ever-shifting contexts. This seems like a fairly obvious statement, but when one considers the range of factors that affect writing programs—institutional sites, budgets, intellectual changes in the field, staffing—and the ways programs themselves grow and shift, it's clear that many variables come into play to create an array of challenges and opportunities. A brief narrative of the history of UC Santa Barbara's Writing Program demonstrates some distinct challenges we have faced, along with specific responses and proactive strategies that have helped us grow. Moreover, the Great Recession of 2008 provides a useful frame for examining the effectiveness, resiliency, and flexibility of these responses and strategies.

As one of the oldest independent writing programs (IWPs) in the United States, the UCSB Writing Program has worked through challenges that other independent writing programs can expect to face. While all institutional contexts are local, and to some extent idiosyncratic, UC Santa Barbara's strategies for responding to those changing contexts might serve as useful models for other programs. Established as an independent unit in 1993 (and operating as a quasi-independent program since 1987), UCSB's Writing Program has evolved in what we retrospectively identify as five different periods. Several important constants have remained during these periods: the program has always been staffed almost entirely by non-tenure-track lecturers, it has always been in the division of Humanities and Fine Arts (HFA) within the College of Letters and Science, and its broader institutional context is a research-intensive institution with a diverse student body and a commitment to undergraduate education.

The first stage of its history, when the Writing Program separated from the English Department, involved the consolidation of existing

DOI: 10.7330/9781607328957.c010

programs in the establishment of *a unit focused on serving the campus.*
This new unit brought together the Freshman English Program, a two-
course, literature-based, lower-division writing sequence; the Program of
Intensive English, which offered lower-division writing courses specifically for Educational Opportunity Program (EOP) (i.e., low-income and
underrepresented) students; and the Interdisciplinary Writing Program,
which offered technical writing and upper-division adjunct writing
courses in connection with academic courses in a variety of disciplines.
The administrative structure of the new program also distanced it from
the English Department: there was a director who reported not to the
chair of English but rather to the provost and an oversight committee
composed of tenured faculty, the majority of whom were from departments other than English. In terms of curriculum, too, Writing Program
courses continued to move from a literature-based approach to teaching
writing as a process and addressing various contexts for writing.

The initial separation from the English Department was spurred in
part by the changing professional orientation of the lecturers who were
teaching writing in these three units: away from literature and toward
composition. Having fifty lecturers housed in the English Department
made less sense, as the lecturers' professional interests diverged from
those of the English faculty. In turn, the establishment of an independent writing program facilitated further pedagogical developments and
professional growth in composition.

Still, the Writing Program was largely viewed in its early years as a
service unit whose primary mission was to serve the university by providing required general education (GE) writing courses. While this service
model is not ideal, as a new unit with only one academic senate member (Muriel Zimmerman, the founding director of the program), a
firm grounding in GE requirements made strategic sense. Zimmerman
worked strategically with campus committees to create a two-course
sequence for the GE writing requirement, with one lower- and one
upper-division course during this period. Because graduate students
needed special exceptions to teach upper-division courses, the upper-
division writing requirement effectively ensured that the Writing
Program would need to hire lecturers with appropriate expertise and
experience; because the lecturers' union had recently negotiated the
opportunity for long-term contracts (and at UCSB, lecturers were generally hired full-time), these lecturers could constitute a relatively stable
faculty for the Writing Program.

Identification as a service unit tied to a university-wide requirement,
then, made sense for the Writing Program in some ways. It ensured

the program's continued existence and meant that faculty would have full-time work, should they desire it. But this identity ultimately separated the Writing Program from other disciplinary departments. Indeed, a 1997 program review commented on the "substantial isolation of the Writing Program from the rest of the campus." This laid the groundwork for the Writing Program's second stage, addressing this isolation by *focusing on curricular and institutional outreach.* The clearest example of this is the extensive revision during this period to Writing 2, the lower-division required writing course. A three-part curriculum for Writing 2, adopted across the program starting around 1996, asked students to write in the genres of the humanities, social sciences, and sciences. Faculty drew on a writing in the disciplines approach and used Behrens and Leonard Rosen's *Writing across the Curriculum* as a recommended text. (Larry Behrens was a longtime faculty member in the Writing Program.) With these revisions to Writing 2, the Writing Program was casting its identity to some extent as a service unit, but one with more direct connections to the intellectual and composing practices of other departments. The Writing Program also established a set of required first-year writing courses designed specifically for students in the College of Engineering. This cross-campus positioning in our lower-division writing courses made sense as a strategy to increase the stability of the Writing Program as well as to align with UCSB's broader emphasis on interdisciplinarity.

With upper-division courses, there was also a sense that increased visibility across the university would bring increased security for a young independent writing program. The program's faculty recognized that the unit was in a relatively precarious position, with faculty hired in large part to teach only one GE requirement. If budgetary or other considerations mandated cutting that requirement, the Writing Program would be decimated. In these early days, then, there was an attempt to have our upper-division courses required not only by GE but also by majors in different departments. Courses included Writing for Social Sciences and Writing for Humanities, for instance. But the program also urged the Department of Economics, whose enrollments were booming, to require one of just three upper-division courses. Many chose what was then known as Writing 109EC (Writing in Economics and Business Economics), and as a result the Writing Program offered many sections of this course each quarter, far outnumbering other academic and professionally oriented upper-division courses. This imbalance in our course offerings, created by the strong influence of another department, was not ideal, but at the time it was a reasonable strategy to try to embed courses across the university, both to increase our connections to other departments and to protect courses from being cut.

A third phase in the Writing Program's history was characterized by a greater sense of security regarding its own position in the university. Sue McLeod was hired as professor of writing and director of the program in 2001, the first faculty member of the professorial rank hired in writing and a nationally recognized expert in writing studies. McLeod continued to develop the program toward *a sense of professional identity that affiliated it with the larger community of specialists in composition*. As she notes in an interview (http://www.writing.ucsb.edu/resources/history), one of her central goals was to bring the program to the level of national recognition and to help professionalize the faculty with two-year appointments, higher salaries, and funding to go to conferences. During this period, McLeod also worked to refine the procedures and policies by which the program's faculty governed themselves as an independent unit, bringing practices more closely in line with those of other academic departments and articulating them in written internal documents and bylaws. McLeod distributed authority and key responsibilities among senior lecturers and streamlined the hiring and review processes.

The 2008 economic decline marked the beginning of the fourth stage in the Writing Program's history, *beginning to articulate the relevance of a disciplinary framework* (even in the midst of financial concerns). With the financial crisis, the program faced the prospect of cuts, as did all of the other departments in the university—but the program's status as an independent program with few senate faculty members made its faculty, most of whom were lecturers, feel perhaps more insecure than those in other departments. The strategies employed in our first three phases of development came strongly back into play and provided guiding principles that helped the program and its faculty weather the budgetary storm. For instance, the program reiterated its grounding in the general education requirement and its role providing an essential service to the university, both to establish a sense of security and to guide the faculty and program's leaders in making mandated cuts. With the exception of courses associated with the professional writing minor, the program discontinued offering all non-GE-status courses. We also continued the outreach to other departments, that was the focus of our second phase in development, for instance, through our practice of hiring TAs from other departments in the Division of Humanities and Fine Arts (where the Writing Program is housed) to teach first-year writing. As an employer during a period in which TA positions, fellowships, and other graduate-student funding opportunities were being cut, the

Writing Program's value to the missions of other departments gained in importance.

At the same time the program was emphasizing its connection to, and value for, other disciplines, we also restructured our upper-division course offerings during this period to allow curricular space to develop and offer new GE courses. Where we had previously offered one large group of upper-division courses that combined academic and professional writing, interim directors Madeleine Sorapure and Michael Petracca now secured approval to create three smaller sets of courses, each within the program's broad focus of "study of and practice with writing in specific contexts." In Writing 2, the lower-division GE requirement, students learned what it meant to study and practice with writing as a subject. Upper-division GE courses in the Writing 105 sequence focus on study of, and practice with, writing as a discipline and writing in civic and community contexts, courses in the Writing 107 sequence on study of, and practice with, writing in professional contexts, and courses in the Writing 109 sequence (those that were part of the original upper-division sequence) on study of, and practice with, writing in other disciplinary contexts. This reorganization both grew from, and helped to define, the program's identity as a distinct unit and to make more visible its disciplinary grounding in writing studies. The restructured curriculum also drew us back to our third phase of developing a professional profile for the program; the course sets and the courses themselves reflected the expertise of our own faculty and were based on research and models in our own discipline of writing studies. In short, conditions of economic austerity caused us to revisit the structure of our curriculum and to make changes that required no additional financial resources but that left us ready for growth in the future.

Coming out of the Great Recession, Writing Program faculty numbers had shrunk only slightly and only through "natural" attrition such as retirements. The program avoided the layoffs, workload reductions, and furloughs that affected other departments and universities. Because of the reorganization of upper-division courses, the program emerged from the budget crisis with a clearer curriculum and with opportunities to add new courses to each of the three sets. Linda Adler-Kassner joined the program as its director and professor of writing studies in 2009, providing leadership and a voice for the Writing Program across campus and in the academic senate. In this fifth stage of our program's development, we started and strengthened initiatives to *reach out across campus from a position of disciplinary knowledge*. This focus is evident in a number of initiatives the program has taken since 2009. For instance, faculty once again revised the lower-division writing course, moving away from the so-called tripartite model (social science paper, natural science paper, humanities paper) to one where students learned to study and practice with writing across contexts, often through assignments focused on genre study. This revision led to a reworking of the graduate pedagogy course taken by Writing Program TAs, since the course's focus had shifted. Faculty began to offer more workshops and training for other faculty through different organized research units. Efforts like these attest to the shift in focus: rather than "serving" other departments or embedding our courses in their majors, the Writing Program's efforts now focus on areas where faculty members' disciplinary knowledge dovetails with the interests of other departments and units on campus.

A few examples illustrate the point. One example concerns the role the Writing Program is seen to play in regard to pedagogical development for graduate students and faculty. As noted, many of the Writing Program's TAs have historically been graduate students in other humanities and fine arts departments (in addition to students from the Givertz Graduate School of Education, where the composition PhD program is located). These TAs participate in the Writing Program's pedagogy course, Theory and Practice of Academic Writing. As that course has evolved, especially since around 2010, those teaching it have emphasized how teaching students *to learn to study writing*, the focus of Writing 2, is beneficial not only for teaching the Writing Program course but also for graduate students as they teach in their home disciplines. In the same way, Writing Program faculty have begun to offer substantive, research-based professional development opportunities for TAs and faculty colleagues in other departments, working with them to consider questions associated with writing and with writing as a reflection of thinking.

In this fifth stage of development, the program has been hiring additional faculty (including 2.5 senate faculty) and adding courses to meet the growth in student enrollment that is occurring at UCSB and at the University of California more broadly. It has also become possible to expand the curriculum by adding courses, particularly in the areas of public discourse, civic engagement, and science communication. Drawing on faculty expertise and responding to student interest, the program has new courses in Writing and Public Discourse, Science Writing for the Public, Writing for Civic Organizations, and Writing in Community. These curricular developments move the Writing Program's outreach beyond the campus and into civic realms, very much in keeping with the broader mission of the University of California and reflecting a position of relative security for the program itself. That is, outreach to local communities and to broader public contexts is grounded in research in our discipline as well as in priorities of the social and cultural moment.

Continuing earlier efforts to increase our program's national profile, faculty and leadership have also developed programs to support professional activities in a variety of ways. Most notably, each year the program sets a portion of revenue generated primarily by summer session courses for travel and research grants for Writing Program faculty. In the past few years, between $12,000 and $14,000 in grants have gone primarily to support faculty members as they travel to conferences to give presentations. This funding supplements money lecturers can receive from a university-wide program. Taken together, these funds enable lecturers to develop and disseminate research that enriches their teaching, which, in turn, serves as an important measure of the Writing Program's fit within an R1 university. The program has robust participation at national and local conferences and is able to hire, as lecturers, new faculty who have PhDs in writing studies, rhetoric composition, professional writing, and other related fields. In recognition of our professional profile, as well as our strong and developing curriculum, the program received the Conference on College Composition and Communication Certificate of Excellence in 2014.

Looking at the more than twenty-five-year history of the UCSB Writing Program as an independent writing program, it is clear that it isn't only during times of budgetary crisis that independent writing programs need to be concerned with effectively positioning themselves in their institutions and for their stakeholders. Different strategies are suited for different times and contexts, and writing programs need to be attentive and responsive to changes in the intellectual and administrative climate, both within and around the program. Two significant and ongoing challenges are the relatively new status of writing studies as a discipline and the tenuous status of the non-tenured instructors who do the majority of the teaching, in our program and nationally. The recession of 2008 showed that writing programs can respond to these and other challenges in ways that ultimately strengthen their mission.

REFLECTION

This brief history of the UCSB Writing Program shows that interdisciplinary, multidisciplinary, and transdisciplinary approaches are all in play in the development of an independent writing program. There is no "correct" way for a program to define its relation to other disciplines or reach out to other academic departments and units. Rather, an array of contextual factors—economic, curricular, institutional, students, and staffing determines the most strategic and effective ways for an IWP to define itself and make connections across campus, and these factors are constantly in flux. As the title of this collection suggests, we discover and cultivate the "allies" we need for our programs to flourish in changing circumstances. Having said this, the UCSB Writing Program's history also suggests that the strongest and most intellectually productive alliances come when an IWP can make connections from a position of disciplinary knowledge, when the research and pedagogical interests of its faculty coincide with, and enrich those of, other faculty on campus, and when genuinely rich and mutually beneficial academic partnerships can be built. For this, an IWP needs to be recognized as an equal partner, with important contributions to make to the success of the institution and its students. From this position, interdisciplinary, multidisciplinary, and transdisciplinary relationships are all valuable and viable.

11

THE FUTURE OF INDEPENDENT ONLINE WRITING PROGRAMS
The Department of Rhetoric and Writing at the University of Arkansas at Little Rock

Heidi Skurat Harris and George H. Jensen

Theory without practice is empty; practice without theory is blind. The ongoing challenge is to bring theory and practice together in such a way that we can theorize our practices and practice our theories. This has never been more important than in the moment of complexity. As we have discovered, emerging network culture is transforming the social, political, economic, and cultural fabric of life. The same information and telematic technologies responsible for the shift from an industrial to a postindustrial economy are bringing higher education to the tipping point where unprecedented change becomes unavoidable.
—Mark C. Taylor, *The Moment of Complexity*

Each independent writing program has its own creation myth—its own set of circumstances that rose to a crisis, a period of acrimony, and an explosion of energy, leaving new territory in its wake (O'Neill, Crow, and Burton 2002). The creation myth for the Department of Rhetoric and Writing at the University of Arkansas at Little Rock (UALR) emerged from events that largely transpired between March 23 and May 7, 1993 (Maid 2002).

While tension had been building for years between literature and composition faculty, the catalyst was a departmental election. The chair of the Department of English at UALR was up for reelection. Six new instructors (full-time, non-tenure-track faculty) had been hired the year before, and they felt they had a right to vote. Most of the literature faculty said, "No, that's not what's in the bylaws." One reportedly added, "We don't let secretaries vote." After several months of heated discussion, Provost Joel Anderson walked into a Department of English faculty meeting and announced that he was forming a new department, which

DOI: 10.7330/9781607328957.c011

would eventually be called the Department of Rhetoric and Writing (DRW). Faculty could decide to remain in English or go to the new department. As legend has it, the faculty who chose the latter loaded boxes on their office chairs and rolled their belongings across campus to their new offices.

The first-year composition program and an MA in expository writing (later the MA in professional and technical writing) went with the new department, as did the instructors and tenure-stream faculty who were specialists in composition theory or technical writing, with one exception: one of the technical writers decided to remain in English and did not teach technical writing again for the rest of his career. The literature faculty, fiction writers, and poets remained in English, as did the BA in English and the minor in English education.

Eight years earlier, in her 1985 College Composition and Communication (CCCC) chair's address, Maxine Hairston (1985) had described literature professors as dinosaurs standing around waiting for the weather to change. At the University of Arkansas at Little Rock, a meteor struck, the weather changed, and a new independent writing program emerged from the ashes.

FORGING NEW TERRITORY: 1994–2008

In 1994, ten years before Kathleen Blake Yancey (2004) called for the creation of writing majors in her CCCC keynote address, the DRW created the BA in professional and technical writing (PTW). In a way, this was a back formation from the already existing MA program. The new BA program focused mainly on expository and technical writing. As the program developed during its first decade, DRW added courses in persuasion and editing, which included an array of elective courses like Document Design, Editing for Publication, Writing for the Web, and Writing Software Documentation. By 2004, DRW had a robust BA program with about 120 majors (on a campus of approximately 12,000 students).

In 2008, DRW went through a major revision of its BA degree. With the emergence of new media, the department wanted to embed more technology and multimedia writing into the professional and technical writing program. At a program level, Document Design, a course always taught in a computer class, which exposed students to a wide range of software (e.g., Illustrator, InDesign, Photoshop), became a required course (L'Eplattenier and Jensen 2015). As DRW was revising the BA, it was also developing a proposal for a PhD program in rhetoric, professional writing, and digital media. The proposal for the doctoral program was set to begin a long approval process in fall 2008.

Then the stock market dropped, and the doctoral proposal was put on indefinite hold. The university and the department began to experience a drop in enrollments—in short, the landscape changed. Both the university and the department began to move in a new direction.

DEVELOPING ONLINE PROGRAMS: 2008–16

In the wake of the Great Recession of 2008, the UALR administration was concerned about a number of threats at the national level, which both the chancellor and the provost discussed regularly before university assemblies, the Faculty Senate, and the Chairs Council. Profit online institutions were growing rapidly (Marcus 2016). In 2011, Stanford University offered the first Massive Open Online Courses (MOOCs). The courses were offered for free, which some pundits like Newt Gingrich thought would revolutionize higher education. These events seemed to signal trouble beyond the cyclical shifts between lean and robust budget years, which were typical for most state institutions. When paired with looming budget cuts to higher education at both the national and state levels, these threats seemed like they would redefine the role and mission of higher education at a national, if not a global, level.

Within the state of Arkansas, UALR had been a leader in developing online education. The university's online programs were attracting nontraditional students, which comprised a majority of the UALR student population. It is not unusual for UALR students to have families and a full-time job or multiple part-time jobs. Online courses afforded them greater access to college courses. The university's online population was viewed as a potential area of growth.

In 2012, UALR signed a contract with Academic Partners (AP) to expand online programs in business, nursing, and criminal justice. With assistance from AP, faculty would develop a series of accelerated eight-week online courses, which would rotate in a sequence so that students could start at any point of the academic year. AP would recruit the students and receive a portion of the tuition they generated. In less than two years, the university dissolved its contract with AP, which had recruited only a handful of students.

To compound these concerns, the BA in PTW enrollment declined in 2008. While the program had graduated between ten and twenty students each year between 2000 and 2007 (averaging fourteen graduates per year), between 2008 and 2016, six years saw only single-digit graduation rates (with an average of ten graduates per year). The MA program, however, was the inverse, graduating an average of eight students between 2003 and 2007 and averaging almost double that graduation rate (fifteen students per year) between 2008 and 2016. One potential reason for the increasing MA numbers might be workers returning for their MA degrees as the economy downsized. Also, between 2008 and 2016, many of the graduate courses moved online, so the increase in graduation rates could be, at least in part, attributed to increased access to the program for working adults and those who needed to relocate prior to completing the program.

Part of the university's and the department's motivation to move programs online relates to our institution traditionally being a CCC (car-class-car) campus. Even with the addition of four new dorms since 2008, our student population remains more nontraditional than traditional. In fall 2017, the student population was 43 percent minority, 51 percent part-time, and 70 percent over the age of twenty-four. It was clear that, despite the setback with AP, the university would continue to explore online education, including establishing a fully online campus (UALR Online) in 2015.

By 2015, the DRW had already taught online courses for fourteen years. The first courses in the composition program went online in 2001, and as early as 2006, the department began discussions about creating an entirely online option for the BA and MA programs. At that time, about a third of the department's courses were taught online once a year. It seemed like adding a few additional online courses would be fairly simple.

The migration, however, to both online instruction and, equally important, digital media, even in nonfiction and other areas that might be considered "low tech," spanned about a decade. Some faculty members, those who taught key courses, were reluctant to teach online. Other faculty members were open to online instruction but needed time to train in the technology and pedagogy of online instruction. The development of a schedule that would allow students to complete the BA and MA either FXF or online took almost a year. Tech-intensive courses such as Document Design, Writing Software Documentation, and Usability Testing were so dependent on specific—and often expensive—software (such as RoboHelp) that it meant that those courses could not be easily moved online. Also, many of our nontraditional students still had dial-up internet access and struggled with even low-tech online courses. We did not solve this problem; rather, we waited for technology to evolve. As more open-source and free-trial software became available, and as high-speed internet and synchronous video conferencing and remote-access software became more ubiquitous, we could conceive of teaching Document Design—and other high-tech courses—online. As the cost of technology dropped, our nontraditional students could afford faster computers and faster internet access. Many began to access online courses on their smartphones.

The transition was as much a shift in culture as a shift in technology and pedagogy. This was only achieved through extended discussions in the hallway and in faculty meetings.

Between 2015 and 2016, the Arkansas Department of Higher Education gave approval for the department to offer three fully online programs: the BA and MA in professional and technical writing (already in place as FXF programs) and a Graduate Certificate in online writing instruction (an entirely new program offered only online). While these fully online programs are in their infancy, we are encouraged by the response to these offerings. In particular, the Graduate Certificate in online writing instruction has grown at a pace faster than anticipated. When it was approved, we assumed that we would enroll approximately ten students a year by the third year. In our first full year (2016–17), six certificate students graduated from our program, and total enrollment reached twenty students.

THE UNCHARTED COURSE: 2016–24

The Department of Rhetoric and Writing's online programs seem poised to grow in a neat linear line, but we wonder if the future is linear. Even over the past six or seven years, threats to the future of our programs, our department, our university, and higher education seem to have been coming from multiple directions. We are hopeful that online programs will help buffer us against inconsistent enrollment and economic trends if we continue to view online as new territory. For the long term, shifting modalities or tweaking degree requirements will not suffice. Our growth must be in response to the networked future.

But what kind of network? Centralized, decentralized, or distributed? If we conceive our curriculum less as a linear pathway (introductory courses preparing students for more advanced courses) and more as a distributed network with nodes (that is, areas of learning that might form in a number of different environments—computer labs, collaborative workspaces, self-directed modules, internships, online discussion boards, and so on) that interact in flexible, even surprising, ways, we will fulfill the prediction of Mark C. Taylor (2001, 234), who described a less linear approach to education: "The curriculum will look more like a constantly morphing hypertext than a fixed linear sequence of pre-packaged courses. When knowledge changes and both seminar tables and lecture halls become global, traditional classrooms will not remain the same. Like a growing number of businesses, colleges and universities will become click-and-mortar operations in which the old and new economies intersect and interact in unpredictable ways."

In the remainder of this chapter, we illustrate what a nodes/network independent writing program might look like and how shifting writing programs online facilitates this node/network future. We believe that just as our students increasingly work in digital, global environments, so, too, must our writing programs operate in these flexible, shared spaces. In short, we must practice what we preach by creating distributed digital spaces that engage and retain students who enter our programs at multiple starting points and bring with them their own skills, abilities, and narrative histories.

Independent online writing programs (IOWPs) of the future must consider programmatic designs that include accessible, flexible learning that centers on project-based learning (PBL) among faculty, students, community partners, and other stakeholders. In short, the IOWP over the next few years will need to have three elements to develop a more network-based strategy: it will need to create learning environments that are accessible, experiential, and multidisciplinary.

Accessible

Accessibility is the umbrella principle for the CCCC's (2013) Position Statement of Principles and Example Effective Practices. Specifically, Online Writing Instruction Principle 1 states, "Online writing instruction should be universally inclusive and accessible." Inclusivity and accessibility mean that students of varying abilities, socioeconomic situations, language abilities, and levels of technology expertise are able to participate in online writing classes. Accessibility, including online content that is affordable and accessible by screen readers, is a must. Audiovisual materials should include transcripts. Online writing classes should, as much as possible, use open educational resources or cost-effective resources that can be easily obtained digitally.

Colleges and universities tend to offer online courses in a single learning management system to maximize efficiency. However, for students using a variety of mobile devices, online writing programs need to create learning environments that can be accessed not only through browsers on laptops and desktop computers but also on phones, tablets, or other technologies. Online writing instructors will need to imagine content delivery independent of the limited tools of a learning management system, at least in their current state of development. Our online faculty work in a number of areas that help us move beyond the limits of out-of-the-box learning systems: usability testing and design (Harris and Greer 2016; Greer and Harris 2018), web applications, and open educational resource development. We will continue to explore new mobile technologies for access and collaboration (such as Slack, Google Apps, and free online content developers). Technology can provide access to online students; it can also, we must remember, be a barrier.

Experiential

The positive effect of experiential learning is well acknowledged. In 1986, George Hillocks's meta-analysis of effective pedagogy for writing instruction identified experiential learning as an "outlier." In other words, studies of experiential learning produced such significant results that they could not be blended into categories of other approaches. Technology that allows for synchronous and a-synchronous collaboration provides natural environments for experiential learning because students and faculty can establish partnerships with business, industry, publishing, and the nonprofit sector. Students at the undergraduate and graduate levels in our online programs work with organizations across the country, including our grant-writing students, who have partnered with the Limited Resource Teacher Training Program (Cambridge, UK) and the Victor Wooten Center for Music and Nature (Tennessee) to write grants and funding requests. This distributed, experiential learning allows students to refine the collaborative, digital composing skills they will need in the workplace.

Multidisciplinary

Prior to 2008, universities and colleges explored learning communities as a means of creating connections across disciplines. In the late 1990s, UALR experimented with learning communities, but our nontraditional students, who had significant commitments to family and jobs, found it difficult to register for blocks of classes. Building learning communities is easier with online courses.

The nonlinear nature of the twenty-first-century IOWP involves the interplay of the above elements. For example, an IOWP might focus on accessibility and technology independence and present most or all course content in modules (or nodes) hosted in the cloud. These accessible, cloud-based modules would be multidisciplinary and focused on project-based learning. Online modules can be a way of breaking through the linearity of a traditional curriculum.

DRW has also been looking at Aalborg University, Denmark, which is structured around the principle of problem-based learning (Aalborg University PBL). Students work in groups across disciplines and departments, sometimes in association with community agencies, to address social problems. As stated in the university's mission statement, "The objective of the University is to strengthen the students' skills as regards problem identification, problem analysis, problem formulation, problem solving, communication, cooperation and the evaluation of work processes and the quality of their own work" (Aalborg University 2015).

In the typical semester at Aalborg University, students focus on solving a "real-world" problem, such as how to improve recycling. They take three related courses that provide foundational knowledge, which they will apply to their project. They also take a project course, in which they work in interdisciplinary groups under the supervision of faculty and professionals from the community. By the end of the semester, they produce a proposal (their solution to the problem) that they defend orally.

While DRW has incorporated PBL into many of our courses, we have yet to extend this approach to the program as a whole. It was primarily a problem of scheduling blocks of FXF courses with our nontraditional students. Online courses, however, will allow our students and us more flexibility. In fall 2018, DRW offered a series of courses around the problem of homelessness, one of which was a course in political science and a central text, Matthew Desmond's *Evicted* (2016). Desmond had been scheduled to deliver a lecture on campus and meet with groups of students during the semester about a year in advance, so we were able to build coursework around his visit. While efforts such as this might seems like patchwork compared to the institution-wide implementation at Aalborg University, the students seemed to be more motivated and asked Desmond sophisticated questions when they met with him.

CONCLUSION

In the early stages of developing online programs, DRW focused on providing better access to our nontraditional students. As online course offerings grew, demand for sections offered at 7:00 a.m., in the evening, and on Saturday eroded. These students moved into online sections which better accommodated their busy professional and personal schedules.

Now that online programs have brought access to our students, DRW's next stage of development will be to explore how online programs can bring flexibility to our curriculum. This will mean a conceptual shift from a traditional, linear curriculum to a networked curriculum. We need to view online education as an environment that will be more like the twenty-first-century workplace.

REFLECTION

The networked future of online writing instruction goes beyond transdisciplinarity to question the boundaries of disciplines. Colleges and universities are, in part, still medieval institutions that evolved in reaction to events like the Morrill Acts of 1862 and 1890 by strategically aligning priorities during lean times.

However, the Great Recession of 2008 may be more than a cyclical tick that will resolve itself as long as we tweak structures, such as disciplines, that form the pillars of our institutions. Multidisciplinary and interdisciplinary collaboration are temporary means of spanning disciplines. But for programs born in contention, old wounds and new technologies complicate collaboration across traditional English/writing studies boundaries.

Transdisciplinarity is what Steven Johnson (2010) calls "the adjacent possible," or the space around present constraints where small innovations can open space for larger innovations. Our DWR has used online education as a first step to a networked system of nodes where students are able to pull on a range of expertise and knowledge across traditional disciplinary and geographical boundaries to problem solve in the fast-paced world of the twenty-first century and beyond.

The 2008 recession obscures larger events—the still-evolving technology of the internet, the growing disparity of income and opportunity, the transformation and value of labor, and the skepticism about the value of higher education. To preserve our values and traditions, we may need to explore radically new models of not only how we educate but also what education can be to reconsider whether the boundaries of disciplines are still useful constructs.

REFERENCES

Aalborg University. 2015. *PBL: Problem-Based Learning*. https://www.en.aau.dk/about-aau/aalborg-model-problem-based-learning.

Conference on College Composition and Communication. 2013. "A Position Statement of Principles and Example Effective Practices for Online Writing Instruction." http://cccc.ncte.org/cccc/resources/positions/owiprinciples.

Desmond, Matthew. 2016. *Evicted: Poverty and Profit in the American City.* New York: Crown.

Greer, Michael, and Heidi Harris. 2018. "User-Centered Design as a Foundation for Effective Online Writing Instruction." *Computers and Composition* 49: 14–24.

Hairston, Maxine. 1985. "Breaking Our Bonds and Reaffirming Our Connections." *College Composition and Communication* 36: 272–82.

Harris, Heidi, and Michael Greer. 2016. "Over, Under, or Through: Design Strategies to Supplement the LMS and Enhance Interaction in Online Writing Courses." *Communication Design Quarterly* 4 (4): 46–54.

Hillocks, George. 1986. "What Works in Teaching Composition: A Meta-Analysis of Experimental Treatment Studies." *American Journal of Education* 93 (1): 133–70.

Johnson, Steven. 2010. "The Genius of the Tinkerer." *Wall Street Journal*, September 25.

L'Eplattenier, Barbara, and George H. Jensen. 2015. "Reshaping the BA in Professional and Technical Writing at the University of Arkansas at Little Rock." In *Writing Majors: Eighteen Program Profiles,* ed. Gregory A. Giberson, Jim Nugart, and Lori Ostergaard, 22–35. Logan: Utah State University Press.

Maid, Barry M. 2002. "Creating Two Departments of Writing: One Past and One Future." In *A Field of Dreams: Independent Writing Programs and the Future of Composition Studies,* ed. Peggy O'Nell, Angela Crow, and Larry Burton, 130–52. Logan: Utah State University Press.

Marcus, Jon. 2016. "Can the University of Phoenix Rise from the Ashes?" *Hechinger Report,* March 4. http://time.com/money/4246709/can-the-university-of-phoenix-rise-from-the-ashes/.

O'Neill, Peggy, Angela Crow, and Larry Burton, eds. 2002. *A Field of Dreams: Independent Writing Programs and the Future of Composition Studies.* Logan: Utah State University Press.

Taylor, Mark C. 2001. *The Moment of Complexity: Emerging Network Culture.* Chicago: University of Chicago Press.

Yancey, Kathleen Blake. 2004. "Made Not Only in Words: Composition in a New Key." *College Composition and Communication* 56: 297–328.

12

A COMPLEX ECOLOGY
The Growth of an Independent Writing Program in the Aftermath of the Great Recession

Carl Whithaus and Chris Thaiss

The aftermath of the Great Recession of 2008 has presented a new set of challenges for independent writing programs (IWPs). In the United States, public institutions have wrestled with declining state support and private institutions have seen reductions in funds generated from endowments. Some independent writing programs have faced (re)consolidation or mergers with English literature departments or other humanities units on campus. On an international level, the idea that writing is a subject that should be taught in the university has yet to gain traction in many places. In fact, rather than there being a struggle for writing programs to gain emancipation from a smothering home department, the real struggle may be to maintain institutional support for writing instruction at all and have a "home" of any kind. In our work, it is important to emphasize "independence" from English departments, but it is also important to emphasize what writing programs have achieved toward the success of higher education. By explicitly calling attention to the importance of writing and rhetoric in university curricula, writing studies and independent writing programs have helped build educational cultures where focused, disciplined approaches to the study of writing are valued. The idea of writing being "independent" from English has contributed to that success at UC Davis, but there is also widespread acknowledgment, some of it tacit, that writing—which we view mainly rhetorically in a cross-disciplinary framework—has not only disciplinary integrity but a necessary role at a research university.

CASE STUDY: THE UNIVERSITY WRITING PROGRAM (UWP) AT UC DAVIS

Happily, then, the story about the writing program at UC Davis is not one of a forced reconsolidation with English literature; nor is it the

DOI: 10.7330/9781607328957.c012

story of a fledgling program struggling to survive. We have a robust and growing independent writing program. Yet, after over ten years of being a standalone writing program—with national recognition for our innovation and support for writing in the disciplines—the Great Recession of 2008 and the slow economic recovery afterward have created a new set of challenges for our writing faculty and program administrators. These have included (1) changing pedagogical and institutional practices to best accommodate the needs of our increasing numbers of students from multilingual backgrounds, (2) the impacts of emerging information technologies on teaching environments, (3) the growth of our professional writing minor and PhD designated emphasis in writing, rhetoric, and composition studies, (4) a labor grievance settlement with the local UC-AFT, and (5) being assigned administrative responsibility for the college's basic writing program. As an independent writing program, we have had the flexibility to meet these challenges.

While the larger national and international economy was slowly recovering in the aftermath of the Great Recession, the UWP at UC Davis experienced tremendous growth; this growth affected all areas of the Writing Program but was particularly pronounced in our increased number of English as a second language (ESL)–focused courses. At the same time we were growing from a program of thirty-four faculty to over seventy, we were grappling with increased administrative responsibilities as well as increased teaching duties. A program-level committee system that allowed for wide-ranging faculty participation in decision-making processes was perceived as requiring administrative work from faculty whose primary responsibilities were teaching. Working through the disputes around governance and labor issues was a complex process that involved local UC-AFT representatives, labor relations specialists from the Vice Provost for Academic Affairs Office, and representatives from our dean's office for Humanities, Arts, and Cultural Studies (HArCS). These discussions did not undermine the teaching and administrative effectiveness of the writing program, however. In fact, the years 2015–17 also saw the move of the basic writing program from our Office of Undergraduate Education (UE) into the UWP as well as UWP being assigned an even greater responsibility for ESL instruction on campus. At the same time, our graduate program and professional writing minor have also continued to grow steadily. These successes occurred against a backdrop of a variety of political and funding issues at the college and university levels.

DISCIPLINARY STATUS OF WRITING STUDIES:
DEVELOPING DEGREE PROGRAMS

Still, writing's institutional independence from English at UC Davis has been advantageous because it has allowed writing faculty greater control of the curriculum, degree programs, and hiring and promotion processes. The ability of the UWP at UC Davis to meet these challenges emerges from the local history of our program as well as being part of the national story about independent writing programs. A description and analysis of our decade and a half of independence reveals much that is laudatory but also highlights the complex and sometimes contradictory impulses that have shaped independent writing programs since at least 1985, when Maxine Hairston delivered her keynote address, "Breaking Our Bonds and Reaffirming Our Connections," at the 1985 Conference on College Composition and Communication in Minneapolis.

Hairston's CCCC address and her publication of an expansion of that talk in *College Composition and Communication* coincide with the moment in history when independent writing programs began to appear somewhat more regularly in the administrative landscape of postsecondary education. Peggy O'Neill, Angela Crow and Larry Burton's *A Field of Dreams* (2002) documents the dynamics around this rise of IWPs at American universities. The growing number of IWPs from the mid-1980s through the 1990s was in part a product of an increasing emphasis on professionalization within postsecondary curricula occurring at that time. Bill Readings (1996) has critiqued this trend as part of the diminishing scope and intellectual rigor within university curricula, while others such as Henry Etzkowitz and colleagues (2000) celebrate how universities in the 1990s embraced academic-industry-government connections to enhance entrepreneurial development and technological innovation. Etzkowitz and colleagues (2000) argue that in many cases this shift in university culture had economic benefits. In "Locating Writing Programs in Research Universities," Peggy O'Neill and Ellen Schendel (2002) describe how these shifts in university culture, particularly at public research universities, coincided with the intellectual work being done to more firmly establish writing studies and rhetoric as a discipline distinct from English literary studies. Charles Bazerman's "The Case for Writing Studies" (2002, 32–34) argues that the large, "multi-dimensional story of writing" can best be articulated and studied when programs, departments, and the faculty who make them up place writing at the center of inquiry rather than at the margins, as has happened when writing has been studied in English, education, and linguistics. Bazerman's work as well as other pieces in Gary Olson's *Rhetoric and*

Composition as Intellectual Work (2002) capture the developing status of writing studies as a discipline rather than a sub-discipline within English, education, or linguistics at the turn of the twenty-first century.

In fact, UC Davis in the late 1990s was an environment that reflected many of the tensions discussed in Olson's collection and in O'Neill and Schendel's "Locating Writing Programs in Research Universities" (2002) At UC Davis, the UWP became an independent unit in 2004, when it was officially separated from the Department of English after a four-year process in which the Academic Senate and faculty from across the disciplines were instrumental. The curriculum of the UWP in 2004, especially its division of courses between the lower division and the upper division as Thaiss and colleagues (2016) have noted, had been developed over a period of more than twenty years. This arrangement of courses between the lower division and the upper division reflected UC Davis's instantiation of both lower- and upper-division English composition requirements for all students. The emphasis on professionalization and application noted in O'Neill, Crow, and Burton's *A Field of Dreams* (2002), lamented in Readings's *The University in Ruins* (1996), and championed by Etzkowitz and colleagues (2000) was a lived experience for students and faculty teaching writing at UC Davis in the 1990s.

Since the establishment of UWP as an independent writing program in 2004, growth has been both steady and dramatic. We have roughly doubled the number of courses we offer to undergraduates, particularly upper-division courses in writing in the disciplines (WID) and writing in the professions (WIP). Enrollment growth has sparked roughly double the number of sections we offer. Moreover, independence has enabled us to develop new programs—a minor in professional writing; a PhD emphasis in writing, rhetoric, and composition studies; and (since 2013) direction of writing curriculum for multilingual writers—that could not have happened under the English Department, for which these developments were not priorities. Independence, specifically the ability of the Writing Program to hire its own tenure-track faculty with academic and administrative backgrounds and research agendas in writing studies, made this growth and creativity possible.

To understand our positive take on the value of independent writing programs, we want to provide more details about how writing instruction has thrived in our local context. We offer about thirty different courses that meet the lower- and upper-division writing requirements, other courses that meet general education requirements in "Writing Experience" and "Arts and Humanities," plus graduate courses in pedagogy, second language learning, writing and technology, assessment, and writing program administrator (WPA) work. We have a successful minor in professional writing and a PhD designated emphasis in writing, rhetoric, and composition studies that is taken as a concentration by students in six PhD programs (https://wracs.ucdavis.edu). The minor has had more than 300 graduates since 2009 and has spurred the development of a proposal for a major in professional writing. In "The Undergraduate Writing Major: What Is It? What Should It Be?" Deborah Balzhiser and Susan H. McLeod (2010) sketch out how writing majors ranging from those with "liberal arts" foci to others with "professional/ rhetorical" concentrations have become established in a wide range of departments. Our experience with the professional writing minor—and in discussions with colleagues about establishing a professional writing and rhetoric major—conform to Balzhiser and McLeod's overview of how writing majors are generally structured at universities across the United States. That is, while the UWP at UC Davis would be the home for a professional writing and rhetoric major, views about how that major would work from those outside the program have been polarized between a strong liberal arts approach and an approach that would emphasize the professional and rhetorical aspects of the degree and the discipline. The challenges of gaining support for a new major are complicated because they include participants who are less familiar with discussions within writing studies. In addition, undergraduate majors are connected to the funding model for departments and programs at UC Davis. This model creates competition among departments and, in some ways, provides an incentive for established and well-represented departments to oppose the creation of new majors that might take students away from existing ones.

LABOR ISSUES: WHO TEACHES WRITING

One consequence of the 2007–10 crisis was ironic for the UWP. The worst period of the financial crisis, in fall 2009, forced us to lay off our most recently hired lecturers at the time, as the number of sections we could offer was cut back. An irony of this situation was that those who were laid off included several postdocs from the English department, whom we were obligated to hire each year on one-year terminal contracts as part of the separation agreement. We had been arguing against this policy since 2006, as it continued to infringe, to some extent, on our right to hire our own faculty. As a result of the layoffs of these teachers in fall 2009, the dean of our college rescinded that part of the separation agreement, thus giving us greater autonomy in hiring. Since 2004, we have hired eight tenure-line faculty and fifty-plus full-time lecturers, including two tenure-line hires during the crisis (2009) and many full-time lecturers since the crisis, as the economy has improved. In 2018–19, our program had eighty-eight full-time faculty—seven tenure-line and eighty-one lecturers—as well as eighteen emeriti.

The increase in writing faculty over the last fifteen years is especially significant because all lecturers at Davis are full-time, have strong benefits packages, and have the opportunity (usually realized) for continuing status after six years of one-year contracts. Continuing status means these faculty are reviewed for stepped salary raises every three years, but at no point must they have their positions renewed.

We have weathered the retirements of many full-time lecturers, who had been with us from twenty to thirty years, by adding excellent professors with specialties we need in our WID/WIP curriculum. The Academic Senate completed its first program review of writing as an independent unit in 2011. All of these achievements for the UWP occurred despite the economic austerity measures enacted across the University of California's ten campuses during, and immediately after, the Great Recession. Writing has been seen—and supported—by the UC Davis Academic Senate and administration as vital for students' success as current undergraduates and as future professionals and potential graduate students/researchers. The increasing role of professionalization and applied fields may be lamented by scholars such as Bill Readings, however, our experience shows that a pragmatic, applied humanities approach to writing and rhetoric can support the growth of dynamic undergraduate and graduate degrees housed in an independent writing program.

Growth is not without its own challenges, however; calling our situation "an achieved utopia" at UC Davis in our (Thaiss et al. 2016) *CCC* symposium article about independent writing programs was not done without a touch of irony. As many of the pieces in Justin Everett and Cristina Hanganu-Bresch's edited collection *A Minefield of Dreams* (2016) and in our *CCC* symposium article point out, achieving independence for writing programs can be a fraught experience. For instance, while Dan Royer and Ellen Schendel (2016, 24, 26–32; quotation on 26) describe how the Writing Program at Grand Valley is flourishing, they also map how three different kinds of, or approaches to, writing need to coexist: "The unofficial subtitle for our department remains 'A Department of Academic, Creative, and Professional Writing.'" Discussions among faculty who place different levels of value on these approaches can be a negotiation in and of itself, and it takes time to develop consensus, particularly around how to structure the curriculum within a major (Royer and Schendel 2016, 35–39). But having these three approaches to writing embedded in a single writing program creates a dynamic environment in which faculty and students are not loyal to a narrow view of the discipline of rhetoric and composition but rather engage across these approaches to writing. In the "achieved utopia" at UC Davis, we have had similar discussions with faculty who view the relationships among academic, creative, and professional writing differently than others.

Having these sometimes challenging discussions can help establish a vision of writing and an independent writing program as home to something similar to what Keith Hjortshoj (2016) describes as an "interdependent" writing program at Cornell. For Hjortshoj, the interdisciplinary approach embodied in Cornell's freshman writing seminars during the 1970s and later (post-1986) in Cornell's Knight Institute for Writing in the Disciplines traces a developmental line that moves from WAC/WID toward an IWP. Hjortshoj's naming of writing programs as "interdependent" rather than "independent" is important and emerges in part from his initial training not as a rhetoric and composition researcher but as an anthropologist. For Hjortshoj (2016), the story of the Knight Institute at Cornell—and independent writing programs more generally—is not a narrative that begins with Hairston's work and calls for independence from English literature departments; rather, it is the story of faculty with PhDs in multiple fields coming together in a unit to focus on teaching writing across and in the disciplines. Writing is an epistemological stance, or more precisely, for undergraduate students it is developing a stance toward epistemology, toward knowledge construction, that is rooted in their own emerging understanding of how their discipline, their major, approaches knowledge construction and how writing works within the field(s) in which they are gaining expertise. That is, like the program at Grand Valley State, where faculty in an independent writing program value conversations across academic, creative, and professional writing, Hjortshoj (2016) sees the approach at Cornell as not only providing space for faculty with different backgrounds in writing studies to have conversations but as also actively valuing "interdependent" cross- and multidisciplinary approaches to writing. Hjortshoj (2016) suggests that if the only stance toward writing that is valued in an independent writing program is one in which faculty have PhDs in rhetoric and composition, then the initial, multidisciplinary impulse behind WAC/WID, behind acknowledging that English literature alone does not own writing, is undermined.

WAC/WID-BASED IDENTITY AND PROFESSIONAL DEVELOPMENT FOR FACULTY

One of the ways IWPs have addressed Hjortshoj's idea of "interdependence" and the experiences of WPAs similar to those of Royer and Schendel at Grand Valley State University is by developing program identities thoroughly focused on WID, WIP, or both. In "Part of the Fabric of the University: From First Year through Graduate School and across the Disciplines" (Thaiss et al. 2016, 150–52), we document how a WAC/WID-based identity helped in the development of the writing program at UC Davis. A WAC/WID-based developmental trajectory and identity can help faculty outside writing studies see how the inclusion of writing in an English department primarily focused on literary and cultural criticism is somewhat arbitrary and probably more dependent on the institutional history of US higher education and local institutional choices than on logical mapping of disciplines. For instance, at UC Davis, undergraduate and graduate ESL instruction across speaking, listening, reading, and writing had been housed in linguistics for years before the writing courses were moved back into the UWP before the 2014–15 academic year. The location of the ESL writing courses in linguistics helped us show colleagues in the Academic Senate and administrators that the idea of an ineluctable link between the teaching of writing and the English department had never been subscribed to at UC Davis. In fact, the Academic Senate at UC Davis has long valued a WAC/WID approach by endorsing lower-division writing requirements that emerged from comparative literature and Native American studies as well as English even before the UWP had been created.

While our Academic Senate has been a strong supporter of a WAC/WID approach to teaching writing for over thirty years, the questions about disciplinary identity for writing faculty needed to be worked through at UC Davis, as in many writing programs, particularly IWPs. While some of our challenges were related to disciplinary identity and approaches to teaching writing, our main challenges starting around 2010 were lingering elements from the financial crisis—namely, the continuing decline of state funding for higher education, with some improvement since 2010, and inequities in state K–12 public education exacerbated by California's financial woes. When these financial pressures combine with questions of disciplinarity, independent writing programs can be a point where many tensions coincide. To cite one example, the financial crisis pushed the university to increase the number of international students because they pay out-of-state tuition, even as it was cutting funding for courses for second language learners.

However, as the financial picture has improved in the last six years, a concerted effort by faculty, students, and staff across units convinced the administration to increase funding for services and courses for these new students.

This new plan gave responsibility for ESL writing education to the UWP in 2013. While we look at this development as one of our successes since we are clearly the best unit to be in charge of shaping and hiring for this curriculum, this change was a huge addition to our responsibilities in a short time and without adequate resources. Integrating a significant number of ESL—and, later, basic writing courses—into a large, thriving writing program originally based on WID and an integration of academic, professional, and creative approaches to writing creates challenges around resources and renews discussions about what types of writing and writing instruction are most valued in the program. While we have been gradually getting the resources we need for the international students, we have the ongoing challenge of meeting the needs of an already highly multilingual campus whose students have been underserved by an underfunded public education system that has not yet caught up to the realities of educating a multilingual population. Matthew Abraham and Elizabeth Kalbfleisch in "Symposium: The IWP in an Age of Financial Austerity" (2016) make it clear that our state and university are far from unique in this situation. This only partial recovery of state funding resources is important to point out because recent improvements in funding by the state may obscure the overall huge decline in public investment in education over the years.

LOCAL HISTORY: PROFESSIONAL AND CROSS-DISCIPLINARY FOCUS

It is very hard to separate "other" large challenges from the economy that affects a public institution of higher education. For example, we are continually trying to adapt to ways technology has ineluctably changed writing education. Was tech development separate from the financial crisis or a key part of it? Perhaps this is a moot point. Nevertheless, as a writing department with a professional and cross-disciplinary focus, we face technology-related challenges that will continue to change as technology changes. Whereas we have excellent facilities for teaching with technology and many of our faculty have been enthusiastic, creative adopters of technology-enhanced pedagogy, parts of our curriculum and some faculty attitudes toward program learning goals have been relatively slow to adapt to technology change, although we have developed and are slowly adding hybrid and online versions of our most popular first-year course. Moreover, while we are among university leaders in using features of our learning management system, some faculty are considerably behind the curve.

Writing a history of an independent writing program from the perspectives of the founding director (Chris Thaiss) and the second—still serving—director of that program (Carl Whithaus) is a fascinating yet difficult enterprise. It is made even more challenging when the institutional history you are writing is an expansion on a previously published article. In our case, "Independent Writing Programs Post Recession: Complexities and Discontents in an Achieved Utopia" appeared in the September 2016 issue of *College Composition and Communication* as part of the symposium focused on "The IWP in an Age of Financial Austerity." The article documented how the institutional independence of the UWP from the English Department at UC Davis had allowed writing specialists to have greater control of the curriculum, the hiring and promotion processes, and the establishment of new degree programs focused on writing. That piece traced the development of the UWP from its establishment in 2004 through the tumultuous years of the Great Recession (2008–10) and its lingering aftermath (2010–15).

The UWP at UC Davis continues to enjoy a strong reputation across campus and among central administration. Our national reputation, manifest, for example, by annual recognition for writing in disciplines by *US News* in its Best Colleges issue, lends to our credibility here. Our long history of cross-disciplinary collaboration (pre-independence and since), our strong WAC/WID curriculum, student demand for courses and for our minor, and the presence of our faculty on important committees contribute to this high regard. Our main challenge for the future is to keep building the tenure-line faculty, especially to develop administrators for the diverse facets of our growing program, as well as to diversify further the program's research capabilities.

Writing a chapter that acknowledges these tensions and at the same time points out the program's successful growth as a research and teaching unit highlights how complex the ecology of an IWP can be. Mapping out these dynamics in the UC Davis Writing Program shows how the idea of an "independent writing program" is developing in practice. Key elements seen at UC Davis are the importance of (1) having robust conversations about writing curricula, (2) developing writing curricula that serve the needs of multilingual students at a variety of skill levels, (3) acknowledging the importance of faculty labor issues related to teaching and administering an IWP, and (4) establishing degree programs focused on writing and rhetoric. This case study of UC Davis helps show some of the ways IWPs are re-shaping writing studies, writing degrees, and, more generally, the dynamics around undergraduate education. This chapter tells the story of how the UWP at UC Davis came into existence in 2004, not only survived but ended up thriving during the Great Recession and its aftermath, and continued to evolve as a complex ecology into and beyond 2016–17.

REFLECTION

Since around 2010, writing studies and IWPs have contributed to the development of university cultures in which focused, well-articulated approaches to the study of writing are valued. Whether these approaches to writing should be based in a discreet disciplinary understanding of writing and rhetoric or in a well-articulated interdisciplinary studies approach is still an open question. The answer may be "both." Perhaps the answer will always depend on local conditions, or maybe ten years from now, a clearer single answer will have emerged within the field. In our case study, the four key elements we have identified show how the status of writing studies as a unique discipline has led to tensions around how writing is valued and taught at UC Davis. Titling our piece "a complex ecology" is a way of acknowledging success but also the tensions that exist when disciplinary status, interdisciplinary approaches, and multidisciplinarity are at play and not settled. In our context—and in others with similar dynamics—who gets to determine what approaches to teaching writing are developed across departments and within an IWP are not only theoretical questions but practical ones addressed by program-, college-, and Faculty Senate–level committees.

At UC Davis, our ongoing conversations about writing curricula, multilingual writers, faculty labor, and developing degree programs focused on writing and rhetoric show the ways an IWP can simultaneously value multidisciplinary stances toward writing and work to establish writing and rhetoric as a discreet discipline. In an IWP with eighty-seven full-time faculty, there are a variety of perspectives on writing studies as a disciplinary, interdisciplinary, and/or multidisciplinary area of inquiry. As WPAs, we have both found value in what Allen Repko (2011, 8) would see as integral to an interdisciplinary studies approach to writing; we have tried to value writing studies through developing "a wide array of knowledge domains, work, and educational programs that involve crossing disciplinary domains." The idea of writing studies as discrete from English literary studies has shaped the development of the IWP at UC Davis. But the ways writing studies is different from English literary studies is no longer our major conversation; rather, we are engaged in debating the ways we translate inter- and multidisciplinary frameworks into curricula and degree programs.

NOTE

Portions of this chapter were previously published: Thaiss, Chris, and Carl Whithaus. 2016. "Independent Writing Programs Post Recession: Complexities and Discontents in an Achieved Utopia." *College Composition and Communication* 68 (1), ed. Elizabeth Kalbfleisch, 209–14.

REFERENCES

Abraham, Matthew, and Elizabeth Kalbfleisch. 2016. "Symposium: The IWP in an Age of Financial Austerity." *College Composition and Communication* 68 (1): 173–79.

Balzhiser, Deborah, and Susan H. McLeod. 2010. "The Undergraduate Writing Major: What Is It? What Should It Be?" *College Composition and Communication* 61 (3): 415–33.

Bazerman, Charles. 2002. "The Case for Writing Studies as a Major Discipline." In *Rhetoric and Composition as Intellectual Work*, ed. Gary Olson, 32–38. Carbondale: Southern Illinois University Press.

Everett, Justin, and Christina Hanganu-Bresch, eds. 2016. *A Minefield of Dreams: Triumphs and Travails of Independent Writing Programs*. Fort Collins: WAC Clearinghouse and University Press of Colorado.

Etzkowitz, Henry, Andrew Webster, Christiane Gebhardt, Branca Regina, and Cantisano Terraa. 2000. "The Future of the University and the University of the Future: Evolution of Ivory Tower to Entrepreneurial Paradigm." *Research Policy* 29 (2): 313–30.

Hairston, Maxine. 1985. "Breaking Our Bonds and Reaffirming Our Connections." *College Composition and Communication* 36 (3): 272–82.

Hjortshoj, Keith. 2016. "An Alternative History of an Interdependent Writing Program." In *A Minefield of Dreams: Triumphs and Travails of Independent Writing Programs*, ed. Justin Everett and Cristina Hanganu-Bresch, 63–84. Fort Collins: WAC Clearinghouse and University Press of Colorado.

Olson, Gary, ed. 2002. *Rhetoric and Composition as Intellectual Work*. Carbondale: Southern Illinois University Press.

O'Neill, Peggy, Angela Crow, and Larry Burton, eds. 2002. *A Field of Dreams: Independent Writing Programs and the Future of Composition Studies*. Logan: Utah State University Press.

O'Neill, Peggy, and Ellen Schendel. 2002. "Locating Writing Programs in Research Universities." In *A Field of Dreams: Independent Writing Programs and the Future of Composition Studies*, ed. Peggy O'Neill, Angela Crow, and Larry Burton, 186–212. Logan: Utah State University Press.

Readings, Bill. 1996. *The University in Ruins*. Cambridge: Harvard University Press.

Repko, Allen. 2011. *Interdisciplinary Research Process and Theory*. 2nd ed. Thousand Oaks, CA: Sage.

Royer, Dan, and Ellen Schendel. 2016. "Coming into Being: The Writing Department at Grand Valley State University in Its 13th Year." In *A Minefield of Dreams: Triumphs and*

Travails of Independent Writing Programs, ed. Justin Everett and Cristina Hanganu-Bresch, 23–42. Fort Collins: WAC Clearinghouse and University Press of Colorado.

Thaiss, Chris, Sarah Perrault, Katharine Rodger, Eric Schroeder, and Carl Whithaus. 2016. "Part of the Fabric of the University: From First Year through Graduate School and across the Disciplines." In *A Minefield of Dreams: Triumphs and Travails of Independent Writing Programs*, ed. Justin Everett and Cristina Hanganu-Bresch, 149–74. Fort Collins: WAC Clearinghouse and University Press of Colorado.

Thaiss, Chris, and Carl Whithaus. 2016. "Independent Writing Programs Post Recession: Complexities and Discontents in an Achieved Utopia." *College Composition and Communication* 68 (1), ed. Matthew Abraham and Elizabeth Kalbfleisch, 209–14.

13

BECOMING A SOCIAL FACT
Weathering the 2008 Financial Crisis at the University of Pennsylvania

Valerie Ross, Patrick Wehner, and Rodger LeGrand

Writing programs, whether independent or nested within an English department, are structurally and functionally anomalous in the academy. Disciplines, as the main feature of the academic bureaucracy, produce and authorize similarly credentialed members who are necessarily interchangeable, able to travel from one institution to the next, and, with minor adjustments, perform what they have been trained to do in a department that more or less resembles the one that credentialed them. This is much less likely, as yet, with those who staff writing programs, latecomers to the academy. While those hired to teach or administer a writing program can confidently expect that writing instruction will be involved, little else can be anticipated in terms of administrative structures and processes. So new to the table and so diversely situated and staffed, ours is a field that has yet to even settle on a name for itself: rhetoric? composition? rhetoric and composition? writing studies? or on what credentials are required to teach our courses. Moreover, writing program administration rarely resembles that of conventional departmental governance structures and staffing; in writing studies, being a writing program administrator (WPA) is a career path. Thus it is that writing programs often operate without a net in a bureaucratic landscape that depends for its force and credibility on resemblance across disciplines and across institutions. Unlike their departmental counterparts, writing programs are precariously pluralist organizations expected to serve multiple institutional spheres, each of which has its own writing culture and claims to expertise, its own demands upon and judgments of its institution's writing program.

Given these extraordinary conditions of existence, a writing program is wise to avoid the trap of imagining that its identity is at least as stable, homogeneous, and secure as those of the far better-established,

DOI: 10.7330/9781607328957.c013

predictable, familiar disciplines that surround it. Research on organizational success underscores that for pluralist organizations (which certainly include writing programs), failure to identify and understand their own complexity and uniqueness within their broader institution puts them at serious risk. In fact, Matt Kraatz and Emily Block (2008, 244) argue that the "need to placate diverse external constituent groups . . . [constitutes] a minimum requirement for bare survival." No wonder that Elizabeth Kalbfleisch and Matthew Abraham (2014) put out a call to independent writing programs asking us, like so many Ishmaels, to recount how or whether we had survived the financial crisis of 2008.

This chapter seeks to recount how the University of Pennsylvania's Critical Writing Program emerged from the financial crisis relatively unscathed. It also hopes to tease out some of the strategies and strands of operating pluralist identity as an independent writing program (IWP), including as a pioneer of writing across and in the disciplines, and how an awareness of this complex identity has contributed to our continuing success (knock on wood).

Founded as an independent writing in the disciplines program in 2003, the Critical Writing Program of the University of Pennsylvania was, by 2008, sufficiently stabilized and integrated into the university such that the financial crisis affected our program no differently from the rest of the university. Like other programs and departments, we experienced a budget and hiring freeze during which one of our two associate directors at the time took a new job, leaving us to take up the slack. The increased workload and lack of raises dampened our morale, but then again we were reassured by the absence of layoffs and by the fact that other, far more established departments than ours were struggling with the same challenges.

While always remaining alert to our unusual position within the bureaucracy of a university, we were not especially worried that the financial crisis would trigger the need to dismantle or fold our program back into the English department because by 2008 we had become what Kraatz and Block (2008) term a "social fact," which is to say, taken for granted as a part of the operations of the institution. In a recent volume on independent writing programs, examples of this status can be found in the observations of Dan Royer and Ellen Schendel (2017, 24, 23), who discuss the rise of IWPs as "structural necessities" and note that new faculty at their institution, Grand Valley State University, "may take our existence for granted." While Royer and Schendel point to their status in the eyes of colleagues outside their own department, Keith Hjortshaj (2017, 79–80, original emphasis) focuses on the view from within the

Knight Institute at Cornell: "For me and for my colleagues, I can say that our programs and positions have been institutionally disconnected from the English Department for so long that independence from that field no longer means very much to us, if anything. For me, particularly, it means no more than the necessity of our independence from *any* department or discipline." The key for a successful pluralist organization is to ensure that there is an eye-line match between these two perspectives, such that the view of the program by its members aligns with the view others in the institution have of that program—as an independent entity, for example, or a social fact.

One important step in acquiring and sustaining the status of social fact is to develop and continually refine a thoughtful, well-researched answer to the question, Who are we? (Jepperson and Meyer 1991; Gioia and Thomas 1996; MacDonald 2013; Pratt and Foreman 2000). This demands research by one's program into what is valued and understood about it by each institutional sphere, and all the stakeholders and identities with which it engages, including its own staff and faculty. A second step is continually engaging in routine planning, short and long range, and a third is equally continuous and routine, coherent messaging across the plurality while cultivating strong messages within and outside your program. Our first-year strategy was to hold a series of planning sessions with writing program staff and instructors, as well as meetings with a wide range of stakeholders across the university, to gather information about their history with writing, their concerns, and their expectations of the program. We held our planning sessions away from the office to minimize distractions and allow us to devote a full day to each session. We paid for a meeting room at a nearby hotel and bought an easel and giant post-it note pad that allowed us to tear pages off and stick them up on the walls around the room as we made lists of stakeholders, their values and beliefs, alongside our own about writing and our writing program; obstacles, problems, and opportunities we anticipated; and culminating with our reasonable as well as blue sky goals, where we could expect to be, where we ideally would like to be, by the end of the year, the end of five and ten years, and what we would need to do to get there.

We quickly realized, for example, that we had to get our fundamentals in order before we started hashing out philosophy and mission, for discussion made it clear that these were going to be longer-range concerns. Along with information gathering, our next major step was to figure out ways to identify, recruit, and support our instructors—at that time, graduate students and part-time adjuncts, along with a few standing faculty with a deep commitment to writing. We cleaned up course rostering and the hiring process so that our instructors and staff—but also our advisers and students—could plan for the year rather than engage in the panicked, inefficient, last-minute, semester-by-semester hiring and rostering our predecessors, lacking resources, had been compelled to do. We also began the long haul of advocating for raises, benefits, tech, office support, and office space for our instructors; we took a writing center that consisted of a few undergraduates and fewer visitors, run by a graduate-student coordinator, and, through careful planning and integration with the first-year writing program, built it into a bustling student resource with about seventy tutors and 7,000 student visits per year. We developed a curriculum that was supported by thoughtful training and professional development and a portfolio assessment process to address student concerns about fairness and consistency of course quality and grading. We worked hard to identify stakeholders and their concerns and to fold them into our planning and communication goals. We developed a set of systems, including various kinds of data gathering, and produced regular, data-based reports that we shared with various constituents. By the time the global crisis struck, ours was a self-sufficient, well-functioning operation that provided first-year writing seminars and writing support to all four undergraduate schools and their students and reports that tracked our progress that we reviewed with our constituents, including our instructional staff, so we could all see our progress (or lack of it) toward particular goals. In all of our planning, however, we never anticipated the financial crisis of 2008. Had the crisis occurred a few years earlier or had our approach to program development been more leisurely, this likely would have been a much different account. Financial invulnerability has now been added to our goals, under the "blue sky" column.

We also quickly discovered, in attempting to sort out our pluralist identity, that no short history of writing instruction at Penn can do service to its complexity. A writing program arose in our English department in the late 1950s and took shape during the early 1960s. It was led for a time by Jerre Mangione—famed author of the autobiographical novel *Mount Allegro* and of a well-respected history of the Federal Writer's Project but with no experience in composition pedagogy. The writing course was not a requirement. In the 1980s, composition pedagogy was in the air, and the faculty of the School of Arts and Sciences (SAS) began to debate whether to institute a writing requirement for all College of Arts and Sciences students. In 1982, a Writing Center was established along with a fledgling Writing across the University program,

Figure 13.1. Site of Penn's English Writing Program, the former Bennett College women's gym (1927). Note the rings, which would later dangle over the writing program instructors' cubicles. (From the University Archives and Records Center, University of Pennsylvania)

better known as WATU. Both were headed by the freshman English director. Writing seminars in the Expository Writing Program or (later) the English Writing Program (EWP) were taught by the English department's graduate students, managed by a series of non-tenured administrators, or the occasional assistant professor, and lightly supervised by the department chair. English graduate students were guaranteed at least one year of teaching in the program.

In 1984, WATU separated from the English Writing Program and was funded and administered by the provost's office. Soon after, it returned to SAS but not to the English department. Meanwhile, the English Writing Program was housed on the fourth floor (a former gymnasium, un-renovated, with dangling cables from the gymnast rings still tucked into a corner of the high ceiling) of the English department's building (figure 13.1). Along with overseeing the writing program, the EWP director was given departmental duties, such as assigning graders for the department's literature courses and offices to all English graduate students, including those not teaching writing courses. Thus the organization charged with providing the lion's share of freshman writing instruction for the undergraduate population (now around 2,500 students per year) was essentially the working arm of one department's graduate program.

Three of Penn's four undergraduate schools—the College of Arts and Sciences, the Wharton School of Business, and the Penn School of Nursing—approved a writing requirement effective in fall 1993; the School of Engineering followed in 2001. The vote stipulated that the provost and the dean of SAS would provide a program that offered writing courses rather than courses in English literature. At this time Wharton and the Schools of Nursing and Engineering also voted to allow their students to take WATU courses.

With its mission to teach writing in the disciplines, WATU grew rapidly in its collaboration with faculty-taught courses in the majors—creating a new Writing Center, offering a handful of graduate-student teaching fellowships ("Chimicles Fellows"), and hiring and training graduate students and PhDs from across the humanities and social sciences. WATU's writing instruction took a generally coherent, consistent pedagogical approach and philosophy, and WATU faculty and graduate students identified with both their home departments and the WATU program.

Meanwhile, the English Writing Program began to offer "writing about" courses focused on literary analysis and criticism, with topics, course design, and pedagogical approach determined by individual instructors, the least successful of which were dissertation topics pressed into service as writing courses. The English graduate students who taught these courses identified with the English Department and viewed this teaching as a required and not always welcomed part of their progress toward their PhDs.

Pressure from various constituencies—students who enjoyed the variety of WATU course offerings, departments whose graduate students could not teach in the huge English program and had to contend for a few WATU fellowships, the leaders of the three non–College of Arts and Sciences schools who questioned whether their students should exclusively study literature to fulfill the writing requirement, faculty who felt writing should not be the purview of one department, advanced English doctoral students who did not want to teach composition courses—had resulted in the development of two separate and equal programs, with two staffs, duplicated administrative effort, two sets of course lists, two budgets, two hiring procedures, and two training processes. In their wake, some other departments had also set up small writing programs of their own—including philosophy, linguistics, classical studies, and religious studies—using them to provide jobs and teaching experience for their own graduate students.

Seeking to unify these programs, the deans of SAS spent four years exploring the concerns of the many faculty who believed the obligation and benefits of teaching a required course should be shared. Two external reviews were conducted in the span of six years. The second review issued a report in fall 2000 that strongly recommended the creation of a single writing program. The report posed such questions as: "Does the university want to continue to conceive of the teaching of writing in the split manner described above? Or does it want to resolve this division in favor of a discipline-specific approach to the teaching of writing at all levels of the curriculum, first year included? . . . How does the university wish to organize the administration of the writing program? Will it continue to divide the administration of writing instruction between first-year English department–based courses and the discipline-specific approach of WATU?" The committee concluded: "We believe that the discipline-specific approach WATU offers may be the best philosophical basis for a combined writing program at Penn." The English Department proposed that they merge and oversee the EWP and WATU, but the committee felt that while this would address structure and power, it would not address the more pressing issue of a discipline-based writing philosophy and pedagogy.

In 2003, the Critical Writing Program was created and shifted administratively to the Center for Programs in Contemporary Writing (CPCW), which reports to the dean of the College of Arts and Sciences. The Critical and Creative Writing Programs were provided with offices as well as the Marks Family Writing Center (figure 13.2) and classroom space in a Victorian twin just a few feet from Kelly Writers House, a well-established creative writing hub for students and faculty.

The WATU graduate fellowships were honored and continued. The terms of full-time instructors hired under the transitional leadership of the dean of the college were also honored; at the time, these were post-doctoral fellows on a fixed, three-year term. Most graduate students and adjuncts from the English department who had taught writing seminars were re-hired. However, gone were the guarantees of employment for any department, and critical writing began to phase out its dependence on graduate students and adjuncts. By 2014, all instructional staff were full-time lecturers with PhDs or terminal degrees, along with ten doctoral candidates from across the disciplines, recipients of a competitive fellowship. The Strategic Plan of the School of Arts and Sciences included the creation of a formal promotion track and long-term stability for lecturers in critical writing. Two lecturers were appointed the following year as senior lecturers with joint appointments in critical writing

Figure 13.2. Interior shot of Marks Family Writing Center, University of Pennsylvania, 2016. (Photo by Bryan Lathrop)

and the department affiliated with their PhDs. In 2016, Penn approved the creation of the long-term non-tenure-track position, Lecturer in Critical Writing, which ensures full benefits and longevity. Three lecturers are in the final stages of approval at the time of this writing, and three others have been advanced by the Critical Writing Program and the Critical Writing Committee, composed of administrators and faculty from across the disciplines. A process and set of protocols is in place for reviews at three, five, and eight years and appears in the university's faculty handbook.

Of the many challenges and successes since our program was inaugurated, perhaps the greatest and most rewarding has been the creation of a bona fide writing in the disciplines faculty, with a curriculum focused on achieving the outcomes desired by a multitude of constituencies: faculty across the disciplines, administration, students, employers, parents, our own (and probably most demanding) writing faculty and administration, as well as the many other scholars and practitioners in the field of writing studies whose work has profoundly contributed to our curriculum and philosophy, even though, particularly in past years, it hasn't always been a neat fit with a discipline-based writing program. The need to negotiate this plurality of experience, knowledge, aesthetics, practices, and objectives has made ours a highly accountable, engaged, and innovative program. Our premises and practices are continually scrutinized and questioned, most often by ourselves. It has also led to increasing ease of communication with faculty in other disciplines as we exchange knowledge about what makes our discourse communities alike and distinct and has led to collaborative research with faculty in the Graduate School of Education, linguistics, and STEM fields. Through dialogue, study, and our portfolio assessment process, we have developed a shared philosophy and curriculum across the first-year seminars that instructors can tailor to their individual topics and disciplines. Our curriculum has evolved into a genre that allows us to compare, contrast, synthesize, and refine our collective understanding and findings in what has become a highly collaborative, multiple-tiered process of problem solving. Initially driven by the social and natural scientists on our faculty, and seconded by the turn to data-based research in writing studies, we are creating testable theories and practices that we pilot and vote to incorporate or set aside.

We feel that being housed by SAS and having the program report to the undergraduate dean of the College of Arts and Sciences is an advantage, both because that college has historically been sympathetic to writing and because the undergraduate dean's mission is to support undergraduate students and courses. However, this reporting structure is not invulnerable. For example, a new dean or new program director might wish to fold the writing program back into the English department. We anticipate no such occurrence, particularly since the English department has launched an innovative course taught by its graduate students that introduces English majors to research methods, with mentorship provided by English faculty. We expect that, like other disciplines at Penn that phased out their small writing programs, the English Department will not wish to return to the sizable workload and responsibilities of running a writing program. Finally, and most important, there is a historical institutional recognition that writing needs to be represented by a range of disciplines and a slow but growing recognition that writing studies is a field of study, the instruction of which requires knowledge and expertise.

Rooted in a thirty-year history of writing in the disciplines, the threshold concept of discipline-specific writing is increasingly becoming a received idea at Penn. Our biggest challenges now are to continue to strengthen the ties between the program and faculty across the disciplines, increase the number of writing opportunities for students, and find effective ways to support the professional development and identity of our very collegial, engaged, interdisciplinary writing faculty who have become as steeped in writing studies as they are in their original disciplines. To facilitate this, we have initiated a well-attended biannual speaker/workshop series featuring writing scholars whose research speaks directly to faculty across the disciplines (in recent years, Norbert Elliot, Anis Bawarshi, and Anne Beaufort). Many of our writing faculty present at conferences and write articles and books. Most exciting, a few of our lecturers this year gave well-received presentations on writing in their disciplines at national conferences, and a few have manuscripts under review that are focused on writing. They are creating a hybrid identity and knowledge that equips them, and our program, to comfortably traverse and integrate the pluralist identities of academic writing, leading us to the next leg of our journey.

REFLECTION

Like most forms of independence, that of writing programs is at its core financial, though this is not something we are inclined to discuss: a budget of our own, a seat at the adult table, the opportunity to speak directly on behalf of our program rather than hope it gets successfully and sincerely relayed by an English department chair on our behalf. Having, and advocating for, a program-wide budget brings with it a level of autonomy and dignity that is common and recognizable across the different independent writing programs. But all that is solid melts into air when we fold in writing theory and practice in an attempt to identify "a model" for writing programs. Having such a model is a wise goal, given that universities, like all bureaucracies, depend on templates, models, replication, and formalized processes to ensure the quality, integrity, and interchangeability of their products. Yet another common thread across writing programs is their resistance to uniformity and universalisms in general. "Everything is local," we protest when, for example, confronted with a "universal" rubric; "everything is contextual," "everything is inter/multi/transdisciplinary-specific." Reflecting on our collective findings and beliefs about the local, which is getting ever more carefully specified, we are reminded of Kenneth Bruffee (1987), one of the most inter/multi/transdisciplinary figures and influences in writing studies. He called on us to seek interdependence for ourselves and our students. Interdependence generates "levels of ingenuity and inventiveness" that, he pointed out, most of us never even knew we had. Asserting that the real issues facing educators hinged on social relations rather than cognition, Bruffee saw our job, and that of our students, as learning how to assimilate into multiple communities of knowledgeable peers, how to enter and exit such communities in a continuing process of collaborative knowledge sharing and building. In this way, the remarkable diversity of our writing programs, each finding new ways to express this glorious interdependence, surely is the very model of the future of higher education.

NOTE

Portions of this chapter were previously published: Ross, Valerie, Patrick Wehner, and Rodger LeGrand. 2016. "Tap Root: University of Pennsylvania's IWP and the Financial Crisis of 2008." *College Composition and Communication* 68 (1), ed. Elizabeth Kalbfleisch, 205–9; and Valerie Ross. 2017. "Managing Change in an IWP: Identity, Leadership Style, and Communications Strategies." In *A Minefield of Dreams: Triumphs and Travails of Independent Writing Programs*, ed. Justin Everett and Cristina Hanganu-Bresch, 245–68. Fort Collins: WAC Clearinghouse and University Press of Colorado.

REFERENCES

Bruffee, Kenneth. 1987. "The Art of Collaborative Learning: Making the Most of Knowledgeable Peers." *Change* 19 (2): 42–47.

Gioia, Dennis A., and James B. Thomas. 1996. "Identity, Image, and Issue Interpretation: Sensemaking during Strategic Change in Academia." *Administrative Science Quarterly* 41 (3): 370–403.

Hjortshoj, Keith. 2017. "An Alternative History of an Independent Writing Program." In *A Minefield of Dreams: Triumphs and Travails of Independent Writing Programs*, ed. Justin Everett and Cristina Hanganu-Bresch, 63–84. Fort Collins: WAC Clearinghouse and University Press of Colorado.

Jepperson, Ronald L., and John W. Meyer. 1991. "The Public Order and the Construction of Formal Organizations." In *The New Institutionalism in Organizational Analysis*, ed. William W. Powell and Paul J. DiMaggio, 201–31. Chicago: University of Chicago Press.

Kalbfleish, Elizabeth, and Matthew Abraham. 2016. "Symposium: The IWP in an Age of Financial Austerity." *College Composition and Communication* 68 (1): 173–78.

Kraatz, Matt S., and Emily Block. 2008. "Organizational Implications of Institutional Pluralism." In *The Sage Handbook of Organizational Institutionalism*, ed. Royston Greenwood, Christine Oliver, Roy Suddaby, and Kerstin Sahlin, 243–75. Thousand Oaks, CA: Sage.

MacDonald, Ginger Phillips. 2013. "Theorizing University Identity Development: Multiple Perspectives and Common Goals." *Higher Education* 65 (2): 153–66.

Pratt, Michael G., and Peter O. Foreman. 2000. "Classifying Managerial Responses to Multiple Organizational Identities." *Academy of Management Review* 25 (1): 18–42.

14

MAKING A PLACE FOR WRITING STUDIES IN A CROWDED INSTITUTIONAL LANDSCAPE

Frank Gaughan

Hofstra University founded the Department of Writing Studies and Composition in 2008. At this time, ten full-time faculty (one tenured, nine untenured) and approximately two dozen part-time faculty were transferred to the new department. The rationale for this change included three broad goals: increase the percentage of full-time faculty teaching the two-semester composition requirement, improve the quality of tutoring in the writing center, and develop writing across the curriculum (WAC)/writing in the disciplines (WID) programming. Over the last decade, all of these goals have been met. In 2018, we marked our ten-year anniversary by merging with the Department of Rhetoric, which recently left the School of Communication and joined the School of Liberal Arts and Sciences. This merger will make the new department one of the largest in the School of Liberal Arts and Sciences. The merged department will include fourteen full-time faculty (nine of whom are tenured) and over three dozen part-time faculty. While such administrative restructuring brings challenges, the new Department of Writing Studies and Rhetoric (as opposed to Writing Studies and Composition) promises to create a stronger curriculum for students and more opportunities for faculty to teach in areas of interest.

I served as the Department of Writing Studies and Composition chair during the years 2011–17. During my term, four faculty earned tenure, and our department conducted five successful national searches; the writing center grew substantially in size and scope, and we have developed a minor in writing studies with nineteen upper-division course offerings. Perhaps more important, we have been able to enroll these courses reliably by coordinating our offerings with various university and degree requirements. For example, in 2016, the School of Liberal Arts and Sciences approved a degree requirement for writing-intensive

DOI: 10.7330/9781607328957.c014

courses, with the overwhelming support of faculty across disciplines. Meanwhile, the faculty in the School of Business approved their own requirement: BBA students now complete a two-credit course in business writing, which is offered and staffed by our department. Both the writing-intensive and business writing requirements provide us with ways to connect with students across disciplines from freshman to senior year. None of these accomplishments would have been possible without two critical resources: dedicated and generous colleagues who agree on broad programmatic goals and consistent support from the dean's office, particularly in terms of faculty lines and budgetary support.

If these resources are in place, then the narrative below may be useful if you are thinking about creating an independent writing program or if you are charting a new course for an existing IWP. Throughout this narrative, I aim to illustrate three arguments: (1) independence resolves a few challenges but creates new ones, while others simply transfer to the new administrative structure; (2) the composition requirement (that is, the introductory writing courses commonly required by many US colleges) provides a stable enrollment stream, which is vital to the success and viability of any department, but the requirement does not provide a sufficient platform for growth; (3) collaboration is as important as disciplinarity, a fact that is particularly important when attempting to make a place for an IWP inside an already crowded institutional landscape (Carlton 1995; Mendenhall 2014). For example, when our department was established, many areas that might fall under the big umbrella of "writing studies" already had long-standing homes in other departments: creative writing and publishing studies are in English; journalism and media studies are in the Lawrence Herbert School of Communication; rhetoric was a separate department, although the pending merger, discussed below, will change that fact.

The narrative begins in 2008, when the department was created by the dean of liberal arts and sciences after a year-long review by an advisory committee that consisted of faculty, including adjunct representation, and administrators. The decision to create the department was controversial, and the majority of English department faculty (both full-time and adjunct) opposed the idea. As an alternative to a department split, many full-timers proposed hiring more full-time lines in English, including composition specialists, who would ease staffing concerns in both the major and the requirement. Adjunct faculty members were also opposed to the split. For this group, the core issues concerned job security and professional identity. Job security, as defined by the university's collective bargaining agreement, is dependent on seniority and the availability of sections, based on the annual enrollment of first-year students who populate the composition requirement. Hence, the prospect of a split created some uncertainty about the status of this requirement. Moreover, the second half of the composition requirement (English 2) had long been defined as an introduction to writing about literature, specifically the genres of fiction, poetry, and theater—including a Shakespearean play. Accordingly, the professional identity of many adjunct faculty members was strongly tied to the teaching of writing through literature (Tate 1993). Despite the majority opposition, several faculty members made strong arguments for the new department. They pointed to Peggy O'Neill, Angela Crow, and Larry Burton's (2002) collection *Field of Dreams*, which profiled successful independent writing departments. This group argued that the new department would prompt a needed ideological shift as well as an administrative rearrangement: writing studies needed to grow as a discipline distinct from English, and this growth was as important as the goal of increasing the percentage of full-time faculty teaching the composition requirement. In the end, this argument prevailed.

The new departmental structure allowed our faculty to quickly address some long-standing challenges: all ten full-time faculty met the majority of their teaching loads through the composition requirement, and we were able to adjust the curriculum in the second half of the requirement to include instruction relevant to writing across the disciplines rather than writing solely about literature. Other challenges, however, remained: about 70 percent of the new department's faculty members were part-timers, and nine of ten full-timers were as yet untenured. New challenges appeared: as a department now separated from English, we had no major, no minor, or even any course offerings in the general education distribution. Hence, it was not easy to reliably enroll courses other than those in the composition requirement. Early efforts to offer sections of technical writing and business writing faltered because these courses were electives, unattached to specific degree programs or other university requirements. In addition, many students arrive at Hofstra with AP or IB credits, which further limits space for scheduling electives.

Other challenges came with the Great Recession, the height of which coincided with the department's first two years (2008–10). A hiring freeze limited our ability to pursue the other two departmental goals: improvement of tutoring in the writing center and the development of WAC/WID programming. We were not in a position to complete a national search for a writing center director until 2015; however, we were able to make significant progress in this area by drawing on in-house expertise. We developed an undergraduate peer tutor program and a four-credit practicum course. Most of the students who complete this course continue as writing center tutors, so the practicum became one of the first upper-division courses to reliably enroll. Among many other duties, the faculty members who served as writing center director introduced undergraduate tutors to writing center scholarship and prepared them for conference presentations. We also grew the center by attending to the needs of core constituencies. English language learners make up about one-third of the total tutoring appointments, so we focused in-service training on this area. As the total number of appointments grew—eventually exceeding 5,000 per year—we were able to advocate successfully for expanded space. Efforts to develop a WAC/WID program were more challenging than those associated with writing center development. After all, the writing center provides students with a free service and clear potential benefits, but a successful WAC/WID program requires many faculty members from across disciplines to coordinate their pedagogical energies. This is no easy task under the best of circumstances (McLeod and Soven 2006; Coles 1991). The challenge became even more difficult when the Great Recession prompted the closing of the Center for Teaching and Scholarly Excellence. This center had been our best avenue for connecting with faculty in other departments; the center also included a budget for faculty stipends, printing and promotion, food—in short, all of the items that would support a growing WAC effort.

As the department worked to address these various challenges, it became clear that the two-course composition requirement was at the center of many of the issues we faced (Harris 2000; Horner 2015). In some ways, the six-credit requirement suggested to others around the university that WAC programming was unnecessary because students were already receiving adequate writing instruction. Hence, a reduction in the size of the requirement, either through directed self-placement or other means, might have had the effect of placing more emphasis on WAC initiatives. However, without the requirement as currently designed, the department would not have a reason to exist. As an illustration, consider the fall 2008 schedule, when 100 percent of our course offerings consisted of required composition. While the requirement offered a reliable enrollment stream, it did not translate to enrollment in other types of offerings. Course enrollments, then, become our most pressing problem. Our faculty continues to enjoy teaching classes in the requirement, but we recognize the importance of defining academic writing—and writing studies—in more expansive and accurate ways

Table 14.1. Hofstra University minor in writing studies and composition (circa 2011)

Category 1: Professional Writing
Business Communication
Technical Communication
Category 2: Composition and Rhetoric
Grammar[XL]
Structure of English
Advanced Essay Writing
Public Writing, Private Lives[D]
Category 3: New Media Literacy
From Pictograph to Pixels: The Impact of Technologies on Literacies[D]
Navigating the Information Ocean: Research, Writing, and the Web[D]

[D] Meets general education distribution requirements.

[XL] Cross-listed with English department offering, offers credit toward the English major.

(Adler-Kassner and Wardle 2015). We also knew that prospective new faculty hires would question the viability of a department dedicated exclusively to two entry-level courses. In time, it seemed likely that academic administrators would begin to wonder about our viability as well.

In response to these issues, the department established a minor in 2011 (table 14.1). Students were required to take eighteen credits, a standard typical of most minors at Hofstra. We also required students to take courses in at least two of three categories.

We did not expect a large influx of minors, but the program above allowed the department to market its courses as a package and increase our visibility among students and colleagues. Three of the courses, marked with "D" above, allowed us to participate in the university's distribution requirements. For this reason, the courses enrolled more reliably than they would have otherwise. In addition, the grammar course is cross-listed with an identical offering in the English department. (In other words, both departments share the course and coordinate staffing needs.) As we moved more upper-division courses into the schedule, we soon learned the importance of placing them within a reliable enrollment stream. Some departments rely on their majors and minors for this purpose; however, we do not have a major and even when we do establish one, it will be unlikely to enroll in numbers large enough to sustain multiple offerings. For this reason, I emphasize collaboration alongside disciplinarity. Here again, institutional context matters. When the new department was established, the university was in the process of

Table 14.2. Hofstra University minor in writing studies and composition (circa 2017)

Category 1: Professional Writing
Fashion Writing for the New Millennium[S]
Writing for Work and the World
Professional Business Writing[BBA]
Writing for Advocacy[D]
Communicating Science in Public Culture[D]
Scientific Writing
Advanced Scientific Writing[G]
Internship
Category 2: Composition and Rhetoric
Grammar for Writers[XL]
Practicum in Writing Center Pedagogy[WC]
Words and Meanings[D]
Advanced Essay Writing[C]
Examining Narrative Medicine[XL]
Writing against Power and Oppression[D]
Category 3: New Media Literacy
Public Writing Private Lives[D]
From Pictograph to Pixels: The Impact of Technologies on Literacies[D]
Navigating the Information Ocean: Research, Writing, and the Web[D]
Writing the Past in the Present: Nostalgia through Humor and Mourning[D]
Composing for Change in the Digital Age

[D] Meets general education distribution requirements.

[S] Participates in first-year seminar program.

[XL] Cross-listed with English department offering, offers credit toward the English major.

[BBA] Degree requirement for BBA students.

[G] Designed for selected graduate students in STEM fields, XL with biology

[C] May fulfill second half of the required composition sequence.

[WC] Gateway for undergraduate peer tutors.

bolstering overall enrollments through an impressive array of programs designed to attract students interested in STEM fields. If the department was to be successful, we would need to hire faculty and develop course offerings for this growing population.

With the above needs in mind, table 14.2 shows how the minor has developed since 2011. Of the nineteen courses in the minor, fifteen

have a reliable enrollment stream, and we look to create new partnerships where possible. General education requirements are clearly
important—eight of the fifteen courses meet this category—but they
are not the only options. The English department has proved to be
an important collaborator. We designed a second cross-listed course
(Examining Narrative Medicine), and we are working on a third, which
will be organized around the digital humanities. We also worked closely
with the School of Business to design Professional Business Writing,
which meets the needs of the BBA students. Finally, four of the new
courses address the needs of STEM students, including Advanced
Scientific Writing, which is cross-listed with the biology department.

These expanded course offerings also help us address some problems
associated with the concentration of adjunct labor in the composition
requirement. Of the nineteen courses above, five have been taught by
adjunct faculty. In fact, the Fashion Writing course was designed by an
adjunct faculty member. Still, our full-time to part-time ratio remains
about what it was when we began, and the core issues of inadequate parttime wages and job security remain. Working conditions are negotiated
at collective bargaining, so there are limits to what a single department
can accomplish. We can, however, ensure that everyone has adequate
office space, a working computer, and access to space for conferencing with students. We also arrange the teaching schedule so there is
a reasonable amount of predictability from one semester to the next.
Finally, we work to make the composition requirement a feature within
a broader writing studies curriculum while encouraging both full- and
part-time faculty to participate in a vertical curriculum of writing studies offerings.

As the national economy recovered, we began to look at ways to
revive stalled efforts to develop WAC/WID programming. In the past,
some efforts in this area had been critiqued as being too concerned
with issues native to writing studies and too little concerned with issues
relevant to other disciplines around the liberal arts and sciences. Faculty
in writing studies did not fully agree with this critique, but we accepted
it, as we came to accept the idea that collaboration is as important as
disciplinarity. This idea may seem at odds with the goal of carving out
an identity for a new department, but the work we have been able to
accomplish with English, biology, and the School of Business would not
have been possible without a flexible approach to curriculum design.
The same approach proved important for the success of the writingintensive degree requirement—our primary achievement in WAC/WID
programming. This requirement calls for all BA students to take two

courses designated "writing-intensive" to earn their degree. The courses are to be taken after the introductory composition courses, and the writing-intensive requirement may be fulfilled in the major or in general education classes. Hofstra is a late arrival to this type of program, but the existence of so many excellent models around the country allowed for relatively quick passage of such a significant degree requirement (Condon and Rutz 2012; Thaiss and Porter 2010). Moreover, the fact of the new requirement sets the stage for the development of other WAC-based initiatives, including the kinds of conversations about teaching and student writing that emerge from the needs of faculty who are teaching writing in the context of their respective disciplines.

The pending merger with rhetoric sets the stage for us to consider the development of a major as well as a graduate program. Here especially, collaboration will prove as important as disciplinarity. Rhetoric and writing studies are closely aligned fields, but the rhetoric faculty in this particular context trace their backgrounds to departments of speech communication or communication studies. The writing studies faculty members are, to varying degrees, trained in English departments, although many specialized at the PhD level in fields ranging from literacy and social practice to scientific and technical communication. From a distance, these differences seem insignificant. However, as we start to imagine a major in this merged department, the distinctions become more relevant. For example, to what extent should a BA degree in writing studies and rhetoric prepare students for a specific vocational orientation? To what extent should the curriculum foster a critical consciousness? How do these orientations forge a productive partnership, particularly in the face of the explicitly vocational aspirations of students and the mandate to ensure enrollment in classes?

As we begin work in our newly merged department, these questions will not be resolved so much as lived through, but we begin now as we did nearly ten years ago: with generous colleagues and consistent support from upper administration. There is much that remains to be done.

REFLECTION

The editors of this volume, Matzen and Abraham, ask that we consider the meaning of independence for our writing programs. They point out that "no writing program or department is ever truly independent." There is some truth to this statement: true (or complete) independence may not be an achievable or even a desirable outcome. Writing studies realizes the significance of its independence through connection with other units in the university and with the broader public. Through these connections, we arrive at *inter*dependence; we deepen our relations with students and other disciplines; we extend the significance of our questions and the reach of our findings.

Our editors also note that independence from English departments is only one part of a broader question about how writing studies interacts with other disciplines and with the university's administrative structure. Again, there is some truth to this statement, as evidenced by narratives in this volume. At Hofstra, the Departments of English and Writing Studies have become important and regular collaborators, particularly in emerging areas such as narrative medicine and the digital humanities. At this early stage, it is hard to say if these collaborations are interdisciplinary or multidisciplinary. The answer may depend more on the personalities involved in any given project than on core distinctions between the disciplines themselves.

Despite the importance of these collaborations, I'm not sure they would have happened in such a productive way without departmental status for writing studies. Above, I argue that collaboration is more important than disciplinarity. While I still believe this statement is true, I'll take this occasion to qualify: if collaboration is to be meaningful, then all parties must have some degree of power, and for better or worse, power flows through disciplines. At Hofstra and many other universities, independent departments make critical decisions about the schedule, curriculum, staffing, and routine budgetary matters. Department chairs represent the interests of their respective faculty to the dean and provost. The lesson? Independence from English departments is not the end of the story or even the main question; nonetheless, independent status remains a critical step in realizing the kind of collaboration that promises success in our future.

NOTE

Portions of this chapter were previously published: Gaughan, Frank. 2016. "New Department, Familiar Problems: The Composition Requirement as Rationale for Independence." *College Composition and Communication* 68 (1), ed. Elizabeth Kalbfleisch, 200–204.

REFERENCES

Adler-Kassner, Linda, and Elizabeth Wardle. 2015. *Naming What We Know: Threshold Concepts of Writing Studies*. Logan: Utah State University Press.

Carlton, Susan Brown. 1995. "Composition as a Postdisciplinary Formation." *Rhetoric Review* 14 (1): 78–87.

Coles, William E. 1991. "Writing across the Curriculum: Why Bother?" *Rhetoric Society Quarterly* 21 (4): 17–25.

Condon, William, and Carol Rutz. 2012. "A Taxonomy of Writing across the Curriculum Programs: Evolving to Serve Broader Agendas." *College Composition and Communication* 64 (2): 357–82.

Harris, Joseph. 2000. "Meet the New Boss, Same as the Old Boss: Class Consciousness in Composition." *College Composition and Communication* 52 (1): 43–68.

Horner, Bruce. 2015. "Rewriting Composition: Moving beyond a Discourse of Need. " *College English* 77 (6): 455–79.

McLeod, Susan H., and Margot Iris Soven, eds. 2006. *Composing a Community: A History of Writing across the Curriculum.* Anderson, SC: Parlor.

Mendenhall, Annie S. 2014. "The Composition Specialist as Flexible Expert: Identity and Labor in the History of Composition." *College English* 77 (1): 11–31.

O'Neill, Peggy, Angela Crow, and Larry Burton. 2002. *Field of Dreams: Independent Writing Programs and the Future of Composition Studies.* Logan: Utah State University Press.

Tate, Gary. 1993. "A Place for Literature in Freshman Composition." *College English* 55 (3): 317–21.

Thaiss, Chris, and Tara Porter. 2010. "The State of WAC/WID in 2010: Methods and Results of the US Survey of the International WAC/WID Mapping Project." *College Composition and Communication* 61 (3): 534–70.

ABOUT THE AUTHORS

Matthew Abraham is professor of English, specializing in rhetoric and composition and the teaching of English. His publications have appeared in *Cultural Critique, South Atlantic Quarterly, College Composition and Communication, Logos: A Journal of Modern Society and Culture,* and *JAC: An Interdisciplinary Journal of Rhetoric, Culture, and Politics.* Abraham is coeditor of *The Making of Barack Obama: The Politics of Persuasion* (Parlor Press, 2013) and the editor of *Toward a Critical Rhetoric on the Israel-Palestine Conflict* (Parlor Press, 2015). His single-authored books are titled *Out of Bounds: Academic Freedom and the Question of Palestine* (Bloomsbury Academic Press, 2014) and *Intellectual Resistance and the Struggle for Palestine* (Palgrave Macmillan, 2014). Professor Abraham is coeditor of the symposium titled "Independent Writing Programs in the Age of Austerity" in the September 2016 issue of *College Composition and Communication.* Professor Abraham's future projects include working on a book manuscript focused on how Edward Said's theoretical and political interventions in the public sphere can produce new critical perspectives on rhetoric and rhetorical theory. In addition, he is developing a book that examines how diversity is defined, takes shape, and is operationalized in the contemporary academy. Professor Abraham just finished a term as chair of the Committee on Academic Freedom and Tenure at the University of Arizona.

Linda Adler-Kassner is professor of writing, associate dean of undergraduate education, and faculty director of the Center for Innovative Teaching, Research, and Learning at the University of California (UC) Santa Barbara. From 2009 to 2015, she served as director of the UC Writing Program. Adler-Kassner is author, coauthor, or coeditor of nine books and dozens of articles and book chapters. Her last book, edited with Elizabeth Wardle, was *Naming What We Know: Threshold Concepts of Writing Studies* (Utah State University Press, 2016). She and Wardle are also editors of *(Re)Considering What We Know: Threshold Concepts, Literacy, and Writing* (forthcoming, Utah State University Press). Adler-Kassner works with faculty from across disciplines on issues associated with epistemologies and inclusive pedagogy that stem from her decades of research on how good writing and good learning are defined, enacted, and assessed, and the implications of those actions for learners.

Lois Agnew is associate dean of curriculum innovation and pedagogy in the College of Arts and Sciences and associate professor of writing and rhetoric at Syracuse University. Her current research interests include rhetorical history and theory, rhetoric and ethics, and the rhetoric of health and medicine. She is the author of two books and has published articles in a number of academic journals.

Alice Batt is assistant director of the University Writing Center at the University of Texas at Austin. She currently serves as president of the South Central Writing Centers Association. At regional and national conferences, Batt has presented papers and workshops about service learning, (dis)ability, and partnerships between libraries and writing centers in learning commons.

David Beard is associate professor of rhetoric in the Department of English, Linguistics, and Writing Studies at the University of Minnesota Duluth. Professor Beard researches the history, theory, and pedagogy of rhetoric as an interdisciplinary formation. His work draws upon traditions in composition, speech-communication, and cultural studies. He has published in journals like the *International Journal of Listening, Archival Science, Philosophy and Rhetoric, Southern Journal of Communication,* and *Enculturation,* among other venues. In addition, he has placed essays in *What We Are Becoming: Developments in Undergraduate Writing Majors* (USUP), *Engaging Audience: Writing in an Age of New Literacies* (NCTE), *Coming of Age: The Advanced Writing Curriculum* (Boynton/Cook), and the *SAGE Handbook of Rhetorical Studies.* With Richard Enos, he coedited *Advances in the History of Rhetoric* (Parlor Press).

DAVIDA CHARNEY joined the faculty of the Department of Rhetoric and Writing at the University of Texas at Austin as a full professor in 1997. Her latest article, on the use of amplitude in the Gettysburg Address, appeared in *Rhetoric and Public Affairs* in 2018.

AMY CLEMENTS is associate professor of writing and rhetoric at St. Edward's University, where she has served on the faculty since 2012. She manages the internship and alumni outreach programs for the major and is the author of *The Art of Prestige,* a history of the Knopf publishing house.

DIANE DAVIS is professor and chair of the Department of Rhetoric and Writing at the University of Texas at Austin and the Kenneth Burke chair of rhetoric, philosophy, and critical thought at the European Graduate School in Saas-Fee, Switzerland. Her work is situated at the intersection of rhetorical theory and continental philosophy. She's the author of *Breaking Up at Totality* and *Inessential Solidarity,* coauthor of *Women's Ways of Making It in Rhetoric and Composition,* editor of *The UberReader* and *Reading Ronell,* and coeditor of *Fifty Years of Rhetoric Society Quarterly* and a special issue of *Philosophy and Rhetoric* on extrahuman rhetorics.

FRANK GAUGHAN is associate professor in the Department of Writing Studies and Rhetoric at Hofstra University. Previously, he was chair of the Writing Studies and Composition Department and chair of the General Education Task Force. His research interests include program administration, assessment, and environmental rhetoric. He coedited the collection *Collaborating (,) Literature (,) and Composition* (2006).

HEIDI SKURAT HARRIS is associate professor of rhetoric and writing at the University of Arkansas Little Rock and coordinator of the Graduate Certificate in Online Writing Instruction. She served on the CCCC Effective Practices for Online Writing Instruction Committee (2013–16) and is a founding board member of the Global Society for Online Literacy Educators. She is the lead editor of *The Bedford Bibliography of Research in Online Writing Instruction.* Her publications include articles in *Technical Communication Quarterly, Communication Design Quarterly, Computers and Composition, Composition Studies,* and chapters in *Foundational Practices in Online Writing Instruction, Applied Pedagogy: Strategies for Online Writing Instruction,* and *Web 2.0 Technologies in the Writing Classroom.*

GEORGE H. JENSEN is professor of rhetoric and writing at the University of Arkansas Little Rock, where he served as department chair for twelve years and currently teaches courses in rhetorical theory and creative nonfiction. His books include *Personality and the Teaching of Composition* (with John K. DiTiberio, 1989), *Storytelling in Alcoholics Anonymous: A Rhetorical Analysis* (2000), and *Identities across Texts* (2002). His memoir, *Some of the Words Are Theirs: A Memoir of an Alcoholic Family,* was published with Moon City Press in 2009. He is currently publishing a series of essays on *The Federalist Papers* on his blog *Democratic Vistas* (www.democraticvistas.com) and *Homo Academicus,* a serial novel about self-absorbed professors (www.homoacademicus.us).

RODGER LEGRAND is lecturer in writing, rhetoric, and professional communication at Massachusetts Institute of Technology. Prior to this appointment, he was director of academic administration for the Critical Writing Program at the University of Pennsylvania. Along with teaching and research, he has six poetry collections, including *Two Thirds Water* (2018).

DREW M. LOEWE is associate professor of writing and rhetoric at St. Edward's University, where he also directs the Writing Center. He has been at St. Edward's since 2008. He teaches courses in rhetorical theory and criticism, as well as general education writing courses, legal writing, and thesis prep. More about his work can be found at drewloewe.net.

MARK GARRETT LONGAKER is professor of rhetoric and writing, English, and communication studies at the University of Texas at Austin. He is the author of *Rhetorical Style and Bourgeois Virtue* (Penn State University Press, 2015) and *Rhetoric and the Republic* (University of Alabama Press, 2007) and coauthor with Jeffrey Walker of *Rhetorical Analysis* (Pearson, 2011).

RICHARD N. MATZEN JR. is professor of writing at Woodbury University. He has published journalism and academic articles and poems and poetry books in a variety of venues. In particular, he published a chapter in *Machine Scoring of Student Essays: Truth or Consequences?* (Utah State University Press, 2006) and an article in the *Journal of Higher Education Theory and Practice, Journal of Developmental Education,* and *inside english.* He was a coeditor and chapter author for *Reformation: The Teaching and Learning of English in Electronic Environments* (Tamkang University, 2007) and the poet who wrote *Going!* (Finishing Line Press, 2017). His administrative experience includes creating an intensive English program and being a writing program director (six years), writing center director (four years), WAC/WID director (seven years), writing department assistant chair (two years), and writing department chair (three years). His current research interests include educational theories, sociolinguistics, and writing program administration. He is currently marketing his novel, *Mona Lisa,* and continues to teach first-year writing and professional writing courses.

CINDY MOORE is professor of writing and associate vice president of academic student affairs at Loyola University Maryland, a four-year comprehensive university in Baltimore and home of one of the country's oldest independent writing departments. Her scholarship over the years has focused mostly on professional development, assessment, and voice in writing.

PEGGY O'NEILL, professor of writing and associate dean, served as department chair and director of composition at Loyola University Maryland, where she also teaches writing and rhetoric. Her scholarship focuses on writing pedagogy, assessment, and disciplinarity.

CHONGWON PARK is professor of linguistics at the University of Minnesota Duluth, where he teaches theoretical and corpus linguistics. His research revolves around the hypothesis that the subtle aspects of formal (structural) properties are motivated by their communicative functions. His research has appeared in major linguistics journals such as *Cognitive Linguistics, Language and Cognition, Linguistics, Studies in Language, Functions of Language,* and *Language Sciences,* among many others. He serves on the editorial boards for the journals *Lingua* and *Linguistics.*

LOUISE WETHERBEE PHELPS is emeritus professor of writing and rhetoric at Syracuse University, where she led development of an independent writing department in writing studies, rhetoric, and composition, establishing the first doctoral program in a free-standing unit. At present, she is scholar-in-residence in rhetoric and writing at Old

Dominion University, where she has taught and mentored doctoral students since retiring in 2009, including in courses in writing program administration. Author of *Composition as a Human Science* (1988) and multiple articles and chapters, she coauthored *Cross-Disciplinary Networks in Writing Studies* (2017).

MARY RIST is professor of writing and rhetoric and chair of the Department of Literature, Writing, and Rhetoric at St. Edward's University in Austin, Texas. A member of the St. Edward's faculty since 1994, her areas of specialty include discourse analysis and applied linguistics.

VALERIE ROSS is the founding director of the Critical Writing Program, Center for Programs in Contemporary Writing at the University of Pennsylvania, cochair of the regional writing program association, PWPA, and an editor of the *Journal of Writing Analytics*. Her current research and publications focus on writing in the disciplines and professions, including an NSF-funded project on peer review in STEM courses, writing program administration, writing assessment, writing and disabilities, and writing analytics.

JOHN J. RUSZKIEWICZ is professor emeritus at the University of Texas at Austin. He taught literature and composition in the Department of English before spearheading the creation of the Department of Rhetoric and Writing in 1993, serving as its chair from 2001 to 2005. He is the author or coauthor of numerous books including *The Scott, Foresman Handbook for Writers*, *How to Write Anything*, and *Everything's an Argument*.

EILEEN E. SCHELL is professor of writing and rhetoric, Laura J. and L. Douglas Meredith Professor of Teaching Excellence, and a faculty affiliate in women's and gender studies. She is the author of six books and coedited collections, including *Gypsy Academics and Mother-Teachers: Gender, Contingent Labor, and Writing Instruction* (Heinemann, 1997) and *Rural Literacies* (Southern Illinois University Press, 2007), coauthored with Kim Donehower and Charlotte Hogg.

MADELEINE SORAPURE is director of the Writing Program at UC Santa Barbara, where she also teaches classes in digital and multimodal composing and directs the multimedia communication track of the professional writing minor. She has been editor of the Inventio section of *Kairos* since its inception in 2006. Her research focuses on digital rhetoric and pedagogy, multimodal scholarship, and information visualization.

CHRIS THAISS is professor emeritus of writing studies in the University Writing Program (UWP), UC Davis. He was the first permanent director of the UWP (2006–11) and also chaired its PhD designated emphasis in writing, rhetoric, and composition studies and directed the Davis Center for Excellence in Teaching and Learning. A member of the editorial board of the WAC Clearinghouse, he also serves the profession as a member of the Consultant-Evaluator Service of the Council of Writing Program Administrators. The author, coauthor, or editor of twelve books, his next book is the forthcoming *Writing Science in the 21st Century* (Broadview Press), based on his teaching of STEM writing at UC Davis. He consults nationally and internationally on writing program design and practice.

PATRICK WEHNER joined the Critical Writing Program at the University of Pennsylvania Philadelphia as a postdoctorate fellow in 2002 and served as a member of the administrative faculty for more than twelve years before returning to teaching and research. His current publishing and research interests are documentation styles across the disciplines and models of the audience used in the media industries.

JAMIE WHITE-FARNHAM is associate professor and writing coordinator at the University of Wisconsin–Superior, where she teaches courses for general education and in the writing major and minor. Her work includes the collection *Writing Program Architecture,* coedited with Bryna Siegel Finer, as well as research articles in such journals as *College English, Rhetoric Review,* and others.

CARL WHITHAUS is professor of writing and rhetoric at the University of California Davis. He served as director of the University Writing Program (UWP) from 2011 through 2018. He studies digital rhetorics, writing in the disciplines (particularly communication in the sciences and engineering), and writing assessment. His books include *Multimodal Literacies and Emerging Genres* (University of Pittsburgh Press, 2013), *Writing across Distances and Disciplines: Research and Pedagogy in Distributed Learning* (Routledge, 2008), and *Teaching and Evaluating Writing in the Age of Computers and High-Stakes Testing* (Erlbaum, 2005). He is the coeditor of the *Journal of Writing Assessment.*

TRACI A. ZIMMERMAN is professor and director of the School of Writing, Rhetoric and Technical Communication (WRTC) at James Madison University. Her research interests are primarily focused on authorship/intellectual property, language and the law, and digital literacies, though her work as an administrator has prompted her to investigate more actively inclusive labor practices and transformative framings of feminist work.

INDEX